Vivienne Belton

Cardinal Thomas Winning
AN AUTHORISED BIOGRAPHY

the columba press

First published in 2000 by
the columba press
55A Spruce Avenue, Stillorgan Industrial Park,
Blackrock, Co Dublin

Cover by Bill Bolger
Origination by The Columba Press
Printed in Ireland by Colour Books Ltd, Dublin

ISBN 1 85607 311 4

Achknowledgements
The author and publisher gratefully acknowledge permission to use photographs from *The Scottish Catholic Observer* and from *Flourish*. Unattributed photographs are from the collection of Cardinal Winning.

Every Blessing,
Dick.
†Thomas J Card. Winning
Chas 2000.

CARDINAL THOMAS WINNING

Best wishes
from Vivienne Belton

For
Mary and George Belton

Contents

Introduction 7

1. The Boy 11

2. The Student 21

3. The Curate and Postgraduate 32

4. The Bishop's Secretary 42

5. The Spiritual Director 48

6. The Parish Priest 59

7. The Auxiliary Bishop 66

8. The Miracle in Easterhouse 77

9. The Archbishop of Glasgow 85

10. Home and Abroad 111

11. The Papal Visit 124

12. The Pastoral Plan 143

13. The Cardinal 158

14. Crisis? What crisis? 174

Introduction

Tom Winning.

You either love him or hate him.

The controversial Cardinal, compassionate hard-liner, social progressive, theological conservative ...

The fact that His Eminence The Most Reverend Thomas Joseph Winning, Archbishop of Glasgow, has been called all of these things and many more during his high profile career in the Catholic Church indicates that he is a man of contradictions.

He is certainly the most contentious churchman in Britain today. Whenever a religious, moral or social issue is raised in the country, rest assured that Cardinal Winning will have something to say about it.

Over the years no political party has escaped his wrath. For Winning, abortion stands out among all human rights' issues and the Labour Party smarts from the lash of his criticism concerning its attitude to the problem. Describing Labour as 'almost Fascist', in 1996, when a pro-life stand was banned from a Scottish Party Conference, Winning also condemned Tony Blair, the new 'caring' Party's leader, for 'washing his hands' of the issue. 'Apologise to Tony Blair!' Scottish Labour had demanded, outraged that the cardinal should fight with the party which was traditionally the most popular with Catholic voters. 'Why should I?' retorted Winning, who saw himself doing only what his people expected of him: giving firm and unflinching guidance on a serious moral problem, no matter how unpopular that guidance may be.

Others had a more cynical view. 'We've become unwitting victims of his ambitions to be Pope!' was one Labour supporter's response to Winning's tough line.

But 'Be hard on the problem, soft on the person' is the cardinal's philosophy and he proceeded to cause more controversy when he made a pledge to all women in Britain, irrespective of creed or colour, who were considering having an abortion because they were too poor to bring up their babies. 'Don't make the worst mistake of your life,' he told them. 'Have your baby and come to the Archdiocese of Glasgow for help.'

Winning saw this as an attempt to turn the tide against the 'culture of death' as he called it, but the National Abortion Campaign said that the Catholic Church should plough money into sex education and drop its attitude to contraception. What did a celibate know about abortion? The cardinal was merely staging a publicity stunt.

Winning has often had a go at the conservatives, too. He took the government to task during the Gulf Crisis in 1991, when he told the Foreign Secretary, Douglas Hurd, that war was no foundation for peace, and diplomacy not belligerency should be the priority. Thirteen and a half thousand Scots were involved in the Gulf War and Tom Winning, with his anti-war stance, was criticised for undermining their morale. He was undeterred by those who said he was being disloyal to Britain and even when his colleague in Westminster, Cardinal Basil Hume, disagreed with him. Winning, the 'turbulent priest', was meddling in politics again.

Full of enthusiasm at the birth of the new Scottish Parliament in 1999, less than a year later he called it 'an utter failure'. His involvement in a lengthy and highly publicised wrangle with the Executive, as it attempted to scrap the ban on the promotion of homosexuality in schools, had left him disillusioned. Throughout the dispute, the cardinal ensured that everyone knew the church's official moral teaching with regard to homosexual acts and although it had not been his intent, his uncompromising language alienated many members of the Gay and Lesbian community.

He does not set great store by political correctness.

Everyone remembers when he was the only Catholic clergyman in Britain to challenge the Prince of Wales to justify the law of the land which prohibits Catholics from becoming Monarch. It was then, back in 1978, that the media realised just what 'good copy' the Archbishop of Glasgow was proving to be. His frank statements have filled the front pages of many a national newspaper but Winning has blown hot and cold with the press too. In 1996, he described the tabloids as 'the gestapo in Britain in the 1990s' after their coverage of the sex scandal involving one of his own Scottish bishops, and he refused to talk to them.

Some say that Cardinal Winning is a religious bigot, finding it difficult to reconcile his much publicised attempts to promote unity of the Catholic and Protestant churches while still insisting on separate schooling for Catholic children. But to those who demand 'integration' Tom Winning gives short shrift. There is not enough Christian education in non-denominational schools as far as he is concerned: 'It wouldn't be integration but disintegration because we would be integrating with nothing!' he says.

In public, Tom Winning does come across as a very tough customer, the hard, dour man from Lanarkshire. Yet in private he is warm-hearted, shy and diffident about his abilities. He is not highly rated as a public speaker, but is witty and engaging on a personal level. Like so many people in Scotland, he loves football. He has supported Glasgow Celtic all his life and can often be seen on a Saturday afternoon in Paradise, as the home ground is affectionately known, cheering on his team.

Born into a working class family, Tom Winning started life in the church as a young curate and a sickly one at that. He had no ambitions whatsoever. Now his title is 'Eminence' but he has not forgotten his roots. He remains a man of the people, with no time for pomp or ceremony. This is a trait which many Scots appreciate and which could not be better captured than in the words of an old sailor from Anderston, on meeting his archbishop for the first time. 'Oh, yer grace, Ah'm delighted tae meet ye!' the old man said, his face lighting up with pleasure. 'Dae ye know whit ah like maist aboot ye? Ye've goat nae dignity!'

Tom Winning – you either love him or you hate him but you cannot ignore him.

In 1994, a contingent of Scots accompanied the controversial cardinal to Rome, to see him receive his red hat from the Pope. The jubilation, banner-waving and bagpipe-playing in which they revelled, while gathered in St Peter's Square, attracted considerable attention. 'Cardinal Winning's miles better!' was the slogan on one of the flags. Seeing this, newspaper reporters from other countries, at the Vatican to cover the event, were heard to ask: 'Just who is Winning?'

Perhaps this story will provide an answer.

CHAPTER ONE

The Boy

Births:

Winning: On 3rd June, 1925, to Thomas and Agnes (nee Canning), at 489 Glasgow Road, Craigneuk, Wishaw, the gift of a son, Thomas Joseph. Deo gratias.

The house where Tom was born is no longer standing. It was demolished some years ago and an Orange Lodge was built on the site. Perhaps the members will, one day, put a plaque on the wall to commemorate his birth there.

His vocation to the priesthood came early in life. Tom was standing outside St Patrick's Church, Shieldmuir. Six years of age, he held his mother's hand as she lingered to see which of her many relatives and friends she might meet coming out of Mass. The boy had eyes for only two men, Passkeepers, members of the Saint Vincent de Paul Society, carrying canvas bags from the church towards the presbytery. 'What's in the bags, Mum?' Tom asked. 'Bags? Oh yes. That's the Sunday collection money,' explained his mother. 'Who gets it, Mum, the money?' 'Well ... the parish priest of course.' There was a pause. This was the moment of destiny! 'When I grow up, Mum,' said Tom, 'I'm going to be a parish priest.'

Not long after Tom was born, the Winnings moved to a larger house at 511 Glasgow Road and this was home until he was seventeen. Then one of his mother's aunts died and left her property to Tom's father in gratitude for the help he had given to her late husband in his declining years. The aunt's house was spacious, with a beautiful back garden. It was a happy place. His new address was 524 Glasgow Road and it would seem now that Tom was progressing along the right route to the big city. However, there were a few diversions ahead.

Tom's maternal grandparents were born in Scotland but the great grandparents were from Kilmacrennan and Ramelton in County Donegal. On the paternal side, his great grandfather came from County Fermanagh and he married a Scotswoman whose maiden name was Weir and that of her mother was Campbell. Both of Thomas Winning Senior's parents died very young. He, and his sister, were brought up by a grandmother and, later on, by two uncles. Thomas Senior devoted a little time to researching his ancestry and discovered his family was descended from Clan Ranald.

Originally a coal-miner, Thomas Winning Senior joined the Fifth Battalion, The Gordon Highlanders, spending four years in the trenches during World War One. On demobilisation, he found it difficult to adapt quickly to post-war civilian life, as did so many young men of his day. He left Scotland for the United States of America and later went on to Canada. None of the various jobs he had was sufficiently interesting to tempt him to settle down in one particular place. He had seen enough of the big, wide world. He was ready to come home.

Now in his thirties, he returned to Craigneuk in 1924 and married Agnes Canning. Work in the mines and steel works was not plentiful but he had found contentment. He was not interested when the new 'Steel Town' of Corby, Northants, offered jobs and accommodation to those Scots who were willing to make the move down south.

Agnes was the second youngest child of a family of sixteen brothers and sisters. Thomas had only one sister and, in getting married, he acquired a record number of in-laws in one fell swoop! As a child, Agnes had been fairly delicate but gained in strength as she grew older and helped to bring up the family of an elder sister who was quite well-off.

Tom Junior's earliest memories as a child are of his sister Margaret with scarlet fever. At that time, children who contracted this disease were taken into the isolation hospital for up to six weeks. Only if they were in danger of dying were parents allowed in to see them. Agnes was very upset and the three-year-old Tom tried to comfort her.

His next recollection was of sitting astride his tricycle watching the family doctor performing a tear-duct operation on his mother in the kitchen. He did not know then that the unfamiliar smell which caused him to wrinkle his nose was from the chloroform mask used to anaesthetise Agnes.

The first occasion on which he and his sister had to have a babysitter was also to remain a vivid memory. This was to enable his mother to attend the funeral of the deceased parish priest, Father Theophilus Delbeke, a Belgian. The year was 1929.

Father Bartholomew Atkinson succeeded as parish priest. He was small and fat and to the young Tom, seemed a pleasant and jovial type of man. Disillusionment came, however, when Tom was about ten years old. He and his sister overslept on a Sunday and missed the Mass specially designated for children at 9.30 a.m. Tom's father was a member of the Saint Vincent de Paul Society (which has special responsibility for the poor) and had been on duty at the church since 8.00 a.m. His mother, preoccupied, had forgotten to wake them up. 'Don't worry,' she told them, 'you can come with me to the quarter to eleven Mass.'

When they entered the church, Father Atkinson came over and was neither pleasant nor jovial as Tom had considered him to be. Rather he was stern-faced and said, in a very brusque tone of voice: 'Why were these children not at the children's Mass?' Mrs Winning, taken aback, turned and hurried the children out of the church. 'We'll go to Wishaw!'

They took a bus and they were greeted at the church door by the parish priest, a tall, slim Irishman, who bowed graciously to Tom's Mother and said hello to the boy and girl. 'What a difference!' thought Tom. It was an early lesson in pastoral relationships.

Tom started his school life in St Patrick's Primary. The Infant Mistress was Kate Whelan and her sister Mary was the Infant Teacher. They were kind women, gradually opening their pupils' minds to the four R's, including religion. They made life so interesting that Tom enjoyed going to school every day and truancy was not a word in his vocabulary.

Tom had one unpleasant experience when he progressed to an upper class taught by the none-too-likeable Mrs Smith. One day, just after interval, Mrs Smith could not find her watch and asked if anyone in the class had seen it. The class jester piped up: 'Please Miss … he's got it!' pointing in the general direction of Tom Winning. Mrs Smith grabbed his arm, pulled him out to the front of the classroom and searched his pockets. All Tom had was a red face. Mrs Winning paid her first and only visit to the school. Mrs Smith found that she had simply misplaced her watch when washing her hands.

With regard to school subjects, Tom had only one difficulty. The Head Teacher of that time, Miss Morrissey, retired and her successor was Mr McCarron, later nicknamed 'Beaky'. Brought round the classes on his first day he asked Tom's teacher who was the best boy in the class. Unfortunately he was off sick. Suddenly Tom found that he was regarded as second-best and the new Head Teacher asked him how many farthings were in three pounds, ten shillings. Tom's mind was a blank. He hadn't a clue. Further questions of an arithmetical nature found him wanting and he was absolutely humiliated. Maths was never to be a strong subject in his academic life.

Miss Crawford was a teacher who regarded Tom as a favourite and often sent him for messages. Miss Biggins, however, was a 'hard nut' and wielded the belt indiscriminately. She did have a class opponent known as JL – Joe Lafferty – who would get his own back by lobbing ink-wells in her direction.

Tom was usually a well-behaved pupil who kept the rules. He did not often get into fistfights but there was a real hard case nicknamed 'Panty' in another class who tried to get tough with him one day during interval. More by good luck that good judgement, Tom got in the first blow, right on Panty's nose, which started to bleed profusely. When his teacher saw the blood all over his jersey she sent for Tom and gave him a good telling-off although she found it hard to believe that Panty had allowed Tom to get the better of him. Tom was not ashamed of what he had done. On the contrary, he was quite exhilarated when he thought of how he had belted Panty. 'He asked for it!' Tom told the teacher, 'He was acting tough!'

When Tom was ten years of age, he was approached by the curate in charge of the choir, Father James Cuthbert Ward, and invited to become a member. Tom's singing ability could be described as average but he soon became a fully-fledged member of the choir, learning to dodge a flying hymnbook when, during rehearsals, the curate would throw one at some poor daydreamer who was not paying attention to his instructions. His greatest fear was that he would arrive for a weekday Benediction and find himself the only person in the choir loft. The arrival of the organist would settle this particular worry although he had no opinion of her ability because she did not pull out all the stops, only two!

At the age of eleven, Tom was asked by the other parish curate, Father Charlie Sheridan, if he would like to be an altarboy, and he served on the altar until he was seventeen and ready to start college. At meetings held every Sunday, the altar boys were well taught: they understood the Latin responses they had to learn and soon knew how to move around the altar without clumsiness, not 'tumbling the book', not giving the bell a passing kick.

Tom liked the idea of serving the priest at Mass. He developed a good rapport with the crusty parish priest who later became a personal friend. But as Tom already knew, Father Atkinson was bad-tempered first thing in the morning and woe betide the altarboys if there was some mishap during an early Mass. His arms would wave about in all directions and the boys soon learned to keep their distance.

Tom Winning's boyhood was a happy period even though he was growing up during the years of the great depression. A year after he was born the whole country came out in the general strike and for adults, at least, it was a sad number of years, but it was good rather than bad times which Tom was to remember. He and his friends would play after school, run around, kick doors and upset some poor old soul, even shout after people on crutches.

They were just boys, 'daft boys' people would call them, running and running and not thinking about the feelings of their elders, whom they bumped into or startled as they whizzed past. Tom did get a fright once, though. A neighbour, Annie Murray, had a crutch and Tom and his friends had been laughing and shouting at her; Annie shouted back and waved her crutch as she held on to a lamp post, enjoying, in her own way, the exchange of abuse. Later that day, Tom met some of the boys again and they told him that Annie had given their names to the police and they were all in trouble. Tom couldn't sleep. He worried all night. Next morning he went to school and the teacher started on long division sums. His mind was closed, all he could see was a big sign: *Police,* and the blackboard was a blur of figures. Long division was not a priority subject! During playtime he was standing at the railings, still worrying away, when he saw one of the boys coming from the Dalziel Co-op store. He was carrying a bag of messages for his mother and must have been off school for some reason. Tom called him over and said: 'What about this police thing?' 'What police thing? Oh ....,' he laughed as he remembered, 'we were only kidding you! Annie Murray wouldn't tell on us!' 'My God!' Tom thought, 'It's amazing how worrying can affect you. Back to the long division!'

Tom enjoyed football although he was not an outstanding player.

In participating in the game, he became aware of the religious divide. Most of the local boys were not Catholics. One of them, a sort of leader, would not have any Catholics on his side for football, rounders or any other team game. Later he fulfilled his potential in the local Orange Lodge. When sides were being picked for a game of football, Tom was often one of the last to be chosen. Aware of his limited abilities, he did not protest too much about this. There were funny moments: 'Ah'm no picking him!' 'How no? Ye'll have to pick him!' 'How?' 'It's his baw!'

At eleven years of age, Tom went to Motherwell Higher Grade, a secondary school. The school colours were originally green and yellow. Two years later the name of the school was changed to Our Lady's High and blue replaced the green and yellow. New buildings were added. At the end of his six years there Tom felt that he had not performed as well as he ought to have done. He was given no guidance on how to study although his parents gave him every facility and he had a room where he could do his homework undisturbed. He liked English and history and also religious education – what he got of it. Mathematics he hated, so much so that he simply made a mental resignation from the maths class altogether. In the evenings he would give his maths homework to his father; he would do it and always got the right answers. How he did it Tom did not know or care. All he did was copy the work into his jotter and present it. He learned nothing of maths.

The teacher of this most dreaded subject was a very fine man but he put the fear of death in Tom. If he had had then the kind of knowledge of their rights that present day children possess he would just have refused to attend the maths classes. However, at that time there was no alternative, nor was it the 'done thing' to complain to your parents.

Tom got on well with the other members of his year group – both boys and girls. During his third year he took German instead of Greek but continued with his Latin studies. When he was about fourteen he told the parish priest of his desire to go to college and become a priest. The advice of the parish priest was that he stay on at school, get his highers and then go to the major seminary. He did not seem to have a high opinion of the junior seminary at Blairs. Tom accepted his advice and did not regret it.

Considering the influences exerted upon Tom during his formative years, his intention to become a priest came as no surprise to those who knew him. His family was deeply religious without being ascetic or fanatical. The church was the centre of his mother's life, his father was heavily involved in parish activities, his aunts and uncles were regular church-goers.

The priests in the parish were role-models too. Morning after morning, for seven years, Tom served their Masses as an altarboy. He grew to love the church and was impressed by those who devoted their lives to the service of Christ within it.

When Tom Winning was growing up there were few professions open to Catholic youngsters in Scotland. When a Catholic answered the question: 'What school did you go to?' in a job interview it was often a case of 'don't call us, we'll call you' as far as many employers were concerned.

The Catholic community was still regarded as an immigrant minority, and, in some sectors of society, its members were treated with hostility and suspicion. Priests had an important role to play not only in organising their people's spiritual lives but also in building up their self-esteem and sense of identity. The priests gave the sacraments to their parish members, but they also helped to run guilds, confraternities, societies and clubs which had both spiritual and social purposes. They spoke out on their people's behalf on many issues and made life a great deal better for the often beleaguered Catholic community. The church exerted an influence on its youth with which nothing else could compare and, for Tom Winning, the life of a priest seemed irresistibly attractive.

Tom's family was pleased to hear of his intentions. His many aunts adored him and when their handsome nephew decided on the priesthood, what greater joy could they have had?

In the meantime, Tom continued to attend Our Lady's High School. Even as a boy he could not help but be aware of the sabre-rattling going on between the big powers, the rise of Franco, Hitler and Mussolini. Very much contrary to popular opinion of the day, Tom was pro-Franco because it appeared to him that the church had got a raw deal from the new communist government in Spain. From time to time there were reports of atrocities committed against priests and nuns and news of their torture and death revolted him. He followed

Franco's campaigns from bulletins on the wireless and, when Barcelona fell after a long siege, he felt it was some kind of triumph for the church.

He was only a boy, of course, but it angered him that seemingly everybody, from the government down, assumed that the whole country was anti-Franco and there were all sorts of campaigns to raise funds for the communist armies. Tom often thought that the Spanish Armada still cast its shadow over the land.

In 1939 there was a papal election following the death of Pope Pius XI. Tom was interested in that because any information connected with the Vatican was always a source of fascination for him. The new Pope, Eugenio Pacelli, who took the name Pius XII, had enjoyed a varied career in the church and he became a hero for the young Tom Winning. He was born in Rome, into a family proud to be of the clerical nobility: his grandfather had been deputy Minister of the Interior in the Pontifical State and made a 'noble' by Pope Pius IX in 1853; his father was a respected papal lawyer. Eugenio himself became a professor of canon law, but it was chiefly as a diplomat that his considerable talents were put to best use. He became a professor of church diplomacy and then, after his consecration as bishop, he was sent by Pope Benedict XV to Munich in 1917. Pacelli's mission was to represent the Pope and deliver to the Kaiser the papal proposals to end the Great War and ensure a lasting peace.

After the armistice, Pacelli was appointed Papal Nuncio in Berlin. He remained there until 1929 when, during von Hindenburg's presidency he was created a Cardinal and recalled to Rome. A year later he became Papal Secretary of State and it was in that capacity that he visited the United States in 1936. There he met Franklin Roosevelt for discussions concerning American relations with the Vatican. Thus, when Eugenio Pacelli became Pope, he was already a personality to be reckoned with in world politics.

Pacelli's experience in Germany made him the ideal choice to lead the Catholic Church during one of the periods of greatest crisis in world history. Seven months after the papal election, the German chancellor, Adolf Hitler, whose name had been mentioned many times by Pacelli in his reports from Munich to the Vatican, ordered the invasion of Poland and soon the world was at war again. The new Pope, despite his many appeals for peace, had been unable to prevent the war, but during the course of it he was instrumental in making the Vatican the centre of innumerable secret missions, peace negotiations and diplomatic manoeuvres.

Pius XII was to receive very bad press regarding his alleged 'silence' about the Holocaust. Tom Winning could never have dreamed that over fifty years later he would be defending Pius: telling students at the Faculty of Divinity at Glasgow University that the Pope had been ready to issue a thundering condemnation of the Holocaust. It had been pleas from Jewish leaders and German bishops, who feared that papal condemnation would result in more slaughter, which caused him to destroy the document which he had written.

The young Tom Winning read all about the Pope in the Catholic newspaper *The Universe* and became a member of its Junior Circle. Reading the papers became one of his favourite pastimes and it was during this period that his father also took up a hobby.

From Tom's earliest years to the outbreak of World War II, his Father was unable to get a job. He was not a lazy man and time hung heavily on his hands. It was during the war years that one of the family relatives taught him how to make sweets.

Local people got to hear about it and started to give him orders. Even the old parish priest, the irascible Father Atkinson, used to send for Mr Winning's marzipan walnuts – despite the fact that he was diabetic and forbidden to eat them. Soon lots of shops bought the different kind of sweets which Tom's father made. The neighbours encouraged him to open a shop of his own but he had no ambition to acquire riches: he simply wanted enough money to educate his two children.

Tom's parents had a tough time financially when he was growing up but his mother was what was known in those days as 'a good manager'. What money she had she used to its best advantage. The newspapers used to feature 'Best Dressed Man' and 'Best Dressed Woman' competitions and, not to be outdone, there was a similar competition in Our Lady's High School. As a result of having no patches on his trousers, Tom was elected 'The Best Dressed Boy' in his class. His uncles and aunts were good to his family and he and his sister were always well-fed and well looked after. However, no money was squandered on holidays and Tom was well into his twenties before he enjoyed such a luxury for the first time.

In 1940, Tom had a bout of pneumonia and, after his recovery, the family doctor recommended fresh air and exercise. Tom's uncle bought him a set of golf clubs which he was to keep for many years. He played at Wishaw Golf Course, sometimes with his uncle and sometimes with his school friends.

At the age of seventeen, Tom passed his highers. Having applied to Archbishop Campbell for admission to the seminary, he went to Glasgow for a preliminary interview. His father accompanied him.

The interviewing panel was made up of old men. One of them was Monsignor Forbes, the Rector of St Peter's Seminary in Bearsden. The others were Canons of the Chapter. One of the men opened a big book, written in Latin, and asked Tom to read a page from it. With all his years of experience as an altar server, Tom was able to read the Latin not with the classical but with the ecclesiastical pronunciation. 'Where did you learn the Latin?' asked one of the crusty old priests. 'At Our Lady's High School and St Patrick's Church,' replied Tom. 'Why do you want to be a priest?' was the next question. It struck Tom that he had never actually articulated his reason before. Just why did he want to become a priest? He sat and thought for a moment. 'I want to leave the world a better place than I found it,' he said.

This answer must have met with approval, because his application was accepted and he was ready to take the next step towards the priesthood. Ironically, he would have to spend the first two years of study at the minor seminary, Blairs, in Aberdeen – the place which his parish priest had so disliked and had encouraged him to avoid.

Tom was excited and sad at the same time.

He was leaving home.

CHAPTER TWO

The Student

All the seminaries abroad in Spain, Rome and Paris, were closed down as a result of the war. That was why Tom found himself at Blairs with, ahead of him, two years of studying philosophy and the prospect of spending the following four years at the major seminary of St Peter's, Bearsden. He was not alone; most of the Scottish students were destined to follow the same programme, with the exception of some Edinburgh students who were sent to Ireland.

Blairs College, as a place, was not much to Tom's liking. He was to take advantage of every legitimate opportunity to get away from it. Not being at home was quite a big change and it is possible that this influenced him to view the college with something of a jaundiced eye. Fortunately, all was not lost! Tom found the classwork most satisfying and had no difficulties passing the examinations as they came along. When he found that maths was not included in the curriculum, he could only commend the foresight of some higher authority!

Despite his initial homesickness, the two years passed quickly for him, mainly, he felt, because the professors at Blairs were helpful and friendly. Next stop – Bearsden!

Tom went to St Peter's, Bearsden, in 1944, to study theology. To him, it was immediately obvious that there was a gulf between students and staff, who kept themselves aloof. The Rector, Monsignor Forbes who was very old, died during Tom's first year and was succeeded by his Vice-Rector, Dr Heary Treanor. In addition, the college was falling into disrepair and, at the end of that session, it was closed down for complete renovation.

Moving again! The students were transferred to St Joseph's College, Mill Hill, on the outskirts of London in October 1945. Tom could only describe the regime at Mill Hill as 'tough going'. They had their own staff and their own rules but to these were added certain rules peculiar to St Joseph's, which also had to be obeyed. The students were not allowed to receive food parcels, they were forbidden to visit private homes or go into the centre of London; all cafés and eating places were out of bounds. The high spot of 1945 for the Scottish boys was getting home for Christmas.

In May, 1946, during the renovation work at St Peter's, Bearsden, there was an accident which led to the destruction of the college by fire. Just at this time, plans were afoot to reopen seminaries abroad – in Rome and St Sulpice in Paris. By October, 1946, therefore, twenty students from different year groups were on their way to Rome, including Tom; others went to Paris and the balance was assigned to a new college which had been purchased at Cardross.

In Tom's student days most trainee priests dreamed of studying in Rome – the centre of the church from the time of Saint Peter. Rome held the most enormous fascination for Catholics worldwide. Rome, the only city in the world with another independent country inside it – Vatican City State. You could walk across this tiny country in five minutes yet in a total area of half a square kilometre are to be found the Roman Catholic headquarters, the world's most famous church and the residence of the Pope – whom Catholics believed was the personal representative of God on earth. To be assigned to Rome meant going to the very heart and soul of the church and for Tom Winning it was a milestone in his life.

From his year group only he and Hugh McEwan were selected. They were not told why they had been chosen. There was an intention to upgrade the educational standards of priests compared to what had been expected of them pre-war and this would have placed greater demands on students in Rome. However, at least two of those sent to Paris were comparable with Tom academically, so good marks were not the whole story.

The majority of men who reach high office and are given key positions in the Catholic Church spend some time in Rome acquiring, along with their degrees, the ecclesial quality of 'Romanità,' a sense of loyalty to the Pope, a sense of Rome as the centre of a church with a remit to spread its message worldwide, a sense of being 'in tune' with church affairs.

Perhaps one of Tom's supervisors had the gift of foresight and thought that he might benefit later from a touch of Roman polish. Whatever the reason for it, Tom thought that next to having a good mother and father, being allowed to study in the 'Eternal City' was his greatest blessing.

In October, 1946, twenty young men, led by Monsignor Flanagan, Vice-Rector of the Scots College, assembled in Glasgow's Central Station for the first stage of their long journey. There were new boys – like Charles 'Donny' Renfrew, just starting life as seminarians, and postgraduates like John McShane. There were also men with 'late' vocations: Felix Beattie had been a soldier before joining the seminary, Stan Smith had been a miner. It was a mixed bunch but by the time they got to their destination they were getting to know one another quite well.

The young boys were thrilled by every aspect of the long train journey which was quite perilous at times, as many of the bridges were of a temporary nature and there was much stopping and start- ing. In Paris they left the train to go for supper in a restaurant. It was night and Paris was lit up with flashing neon signs – something youngsters from Blairs had never seen before. One boy, Stan Quirk, who was about seventeen and just starting off in philosophy, spotted a sign: 'Brasserie d'Esperance.' 'Hey, boys, there's the Band of Hope!' he shouted and they all laughed and Paris seemed a more homely place. Tom Winning was never to forget how guilty they felt drink- ing wine for the first time – and it was not long before they acquired a taste for it.

Soon they were in the outskirts of Rome, the train steaming and whistling and making a great fuss of the last mile or so. Their excite- ment rose. 'There's the Coliseum!' It was Stan again and the boys all rushed to the other side of the train. It was the gasworks! Stan was to regale the boys with his quips for some time to come but, in fact, he did not become a priest.

Finally, they arrived in the great city of Rome. The college Rector, Monsignor William Clapperton, was there at the station to meet them; along with him was Monsignor Gerard Rogers who had stud- ied in Rome before the war and wanted to celebrate the reopening of the college. The boys were taken to their new home in the Via Quattro Fontane – the Street of the Four Fountains. They were now students of the Pontificio Collegio Scozzese, the Pontifical Scots College, a seminary with a long and fascinating history.

The college was founded by Pope Clement VIII in 1600 for

Scottish boys who, because of the spread of the Protestant Reformers' ideas, could not obtain a Catholic education in their own country. It was not meant exclusively for students preparing for the priesthood but by 1616, the Pope decided that it should be reserved for those preparing to work as priests on the Scottish Mission. During the years when Catholics were being persecuted in Scotland, the college sent a small but steady supply of priests back home and it was due to this college more than any other that the Catholic faith in Scotland did not die out completely.

When Tom Winning came to the college, William Clapperton had been Rector since 1922 and was to remain in post until 1960. He had been forced to close the college in 1940, on the eve of Italy's entry into the war, and return home to Scotland with his staff and students. Part of the college was then used as a soldiers' canteen. This was not the first time that the Scots College had been abandoned on account of war. When Napoleon's army invaded Rome in 1798, the invaders occupied the college and turned its church into a stable for their horses!

In 1946, Clapperton found that the college buildings had, inevitably, suffered from wartime occupation. An Italian priest, Monsignor Fidecicchi, had done his best to administer the college in the Rector's absence – and there was also Lorenzo, the college servant. He had locked away the college uniforms left behind by the evacuating students: the dashing purple soutanes, red sashes, black open-coats and black soup-plate hats. Within a week, the new Scottish students were dressed in the full gear – second hand but in remarkably good condition. On their first Sunday in Rome, the boys attended a beatification ceremony in St Peter's, feeling self-conscious but very proud of themselves in their new outfits. They were not alone: the city of Rome was full of seminarians. Each group had its own distinctive uniform, according to nationality. On that first Sunday night, Tom Winning met some scarlet-clad students from the German-Hungarian College. One of them, a Hungarian called Josef Bistyo became a good friend of Tom's. He had been conscripted into the German army during the war. Not wishing to fight for Germany and wanting to fulfil his desire to become a priest, he had escaped and made his way to Rome. When he arrived there he spoke only his native Magyar. Within two years he had become fluent in German, Italian, English and Latin.

Fluency in Latin was just what Tom needed. The theology classes he had to attend every day at the Jesuit Gregorian University were conducted in Latin and so were the examinations. Between classes, he would meet his Hungarian friend regularly and they would chat in Latin. Tom believed that Josef was very much responsible for his progress in the language. The Scots students had only one formal lesson in Italian. There did not seem to be any time for it. Tom and Hugh McEwan were in third year theology and Latin and theology had first priority.

Tom liked the Gregorian University, where the lecturers were all members of the Society of Jesus. His professors were well-known theologians of the day: Lennerts, a German, taught dogmatic theology; Hurt covered moral theology. Flick was a fine scholar of Latin from North Italy. He was also taught by Trompe, who wrote one or two of Pius XII's encyclicals, and Zeppellina, a Spaniard who taught the Tract of the Church for many years to different generations. Not an era of greats, exactly, in comparison to well-known classic names of the Jesuit past, but nevertheless they were representative of the best brains of the church during the period when Tom Winning was a student. Tom had an eclectic approach to his studies. Years later, one of his fellow students, Donny Renfrew, was to say this about him:

> The picture I remember of Tom Winning, when I didn't know him very well, is going to his room in college and, beside his bed, would be a wee table for the books he was reading. He read a lot in bed at night. The rest of us would have one or two books, marked with a holy picture or something, at the pages we were at. Tom would have fourteen books and they'd all have markers sticking out of them. I used to say: 'Can I take away thirteen of those and let you finish one?'
>
> … That is the kind of mind he was. I don't think he goes through a whole book – he seems to be able to get to the essence of one very quickly.

Tom enjoyed mixing with students from other countries but he was not allowed to partake in the social life of Rome. Clerics were forbidden to attend the opera or the cinema. They were not even allowed to go to a football match. Scots College rules were strict. The students could go out in threes, wearing college attire, but they were not allowed to enter a shop without prior special permission. In threes, the senior student had to walk in the centre. If there were four, the senior student walked behind the other three. A student was required to doff his hat to members of staff but, in the city, there were too many clerics about and he learned to salute only those he recognised as bishops and above.

On arrival in Rome in 1946, Tom was the first student admitted to the hospital where a small duodenal ulcer was diagnosed. He had experienced quite a lot of pain during the weeks before setting off for Scots College but he had been determined that nothing was going to prevent him from fulfilling his ambition. The fact that food was still on the ration when the students arrived in Rome did not help his situation. Breakfast was half a panino – a small roll; at lunchtimes the spaghetti was served in tiny portions. Things started to improve on St Andrew's Day. This was a big religious feast and also the day when the Scottish students played their English counterparts in a football match – an annual tradition. That morning, a whole panino was brought in for each of the eleven players plus one extra which was torn to shreds and divided out as fairly as possible. Breakfast sustenance for the big match.

However, there was more to come. For the first time, the students were given a really substantial dinner and they were very grateful to St Andrew, not only for the food but for a day off from lectures at the Gregorian University. After that, meals were better and a lot more nourishing, but it had been tough at the beginning before they were fully organised and, perhaps, better financed.

The students were allowed to enter a restaurant provided it was outside the walls of Rome. It did not take them long to find the nearest point of exit and head straight for a *ristorante*. This became a regular habit, particularly on their obligatory Sunday walks. The black market was still going strong in 1946 and the boys shopped around for the best rates for their money. Food was also a black market commodity but, as they moved into 1947, black marketeering became a dying industry.

The college staff encouraged their charges to broaden their cultural horizons by visiting the churches, museums, galleries and the ancient remains of Imperial Rome, enough for a lifetime of sight-seeing. Tom soon had a number of favourite churches: St John Lateran, St Mary Major, Saint Andrea delle Fratte and the Jesuit Church, the

Gesù. He was particularly fascinated by Michelangelo's statue of Moses in the Church of St Peter-in-chains. This had been intended to embellish the tomb of the artist's patron, Pope Julius II.

As a small boy, looking at his children's encyclopaedia, Tom had seen a photograph of this statue and been puzzled by the caption which read: 'Michelangelo strikes the rock and brings out Moses.'

Moses had struck a rock, he knew, but Michelangelo? When Tom actually saw this magnificent sculpture in Rome, he understood.

In 1654, the Scots College had acquired a villa and vineyard at Marino, a small town twenty kilometres from Rome, perched on the hills known as the Castelli. This served as an out-of-town residence for the students during the boiling hot summer months but they also managed to get away from the city during termtime. Thursday was a day off or *gita,* and an opportunity for a trip. These trips were not without incident however. On one occasion Tom, Donny Renfrew and a few others were on a visit to Sorrento and were waiting for a bus to take them along the beautiful but fearsome cliff road to Amalfi, with its sheer drop to the sea. The boys were held back by a fellow student, always known simply as McNamara, who had disappeared. '… C'mon, we'll go without him..' 'Och, we'd better wait – there'll be another bus in half an hour …' So they waited. Later on that day they learned that the bus they missed had catapulted over the precipice and the only one saved in the incident was a babe in arms. The bus had been full.

Theatre-going in Rome was prohibited to them, but the students performed their own dramatic productions in the college itself. They staged Shakespearean plays and Gilbert and Sullivan operas both at carnival time, just before Lent, and Christmas. The audiences comprised students and staff from other colleges and staff from the British Embassy. The Scots College had a small, quite professional theatre and Tom took part in several performances.

The college was an all-male preserve so the casting of female parts could have been a problem. Students in the American College, for example, were not allowed to play-act as women. The Scots, however, enjoyed the humour of the situation and acted Shakespeare's plays in the style of the Bard's day – when women were forbidden to take part in theatrical performances.

Tom Winning was often cast in female roles and trod the boards as Ophelia, Calpurnia and Lady Macbeth. He took several male parts also – in the operas. Donny Renfrew was asked to conduct *Iolanthe* and the *Yeomen of the Guard*. Later, he was to remember Tom as being something of a problem at rehearsals:

> … it was very difficult, like now, to get hold of him, to start with! With the rest of us, it was easy. We all assembled at the right time but he was always late or something. He would get impatient, just in the same way as he does now, and he'd say: 'Why the hell do we have to do this?'

Nevertheless, Tom was a convincing actor, a real presence on stage. Despite his dislike of rehearsals, he thoroughly enjoyed the actual performances.

Tom was a conscientious student priest but he did have a touch of the devil in him and acquired a reputation as a practical joker. Whenever he saw an opportunity for a prank he would take it.

There was a small square between the college buildings designated for recreation purposes. It was half the size of a tennis court, not much room but the students could play volleyball in the area. Their accommodation was on the third floor and buckets of water were always sitting on the veranda since there were no plumbed wash-basins in the rooms. At recreation time, Tom would come back early from his wash, before the volleyball players had finished and regularly, as a matter of course, empty buckets of water down to the ground floor on top of them. He seemed to have a perfect aim and never appeared to tire of this practice. What the volleyball players felt about it was another matter!

During his stay in Rome, Tom took every opportunity to see Pius XII, about whom he had heard and read so much. He was never to forget the first glimpse of the Pope being carried through St Peter's Square into the Basilica, held aloft in the *sedia gestatoria,* a kind of portable throne, so that everyone could see him. *Flabella* – large fans made of ostrich feathers – were carried to the right and left of the sedia and the Pope was flanked by his Swiss Guards, resplendent in their distinctive uniforms of yellow, red and blue stripes, with wide breeches and leg of mutton sleeves. All the trappings of an absolute monarchy.

Tom was fascinated by the centuries-old panoply which Pius had inherited but he questioned it too. He was learning at university that theoretically it was the college of bishops, with the Pope at their head, who governed the church; but the sight of these bishops, down in the square, waving their hankies up to the Pope as he passed, did not seem to fit in with a vision of 'collegiality'.

Far from being affected by the pageantry which surrounded his office, Pius had, instead, an aura of other worldliness about him. He had an exalted, almost dramatic conception of his role. His final blessing to the crowds in St Peter's seemed as if it had been pulled down from heaven itself. For Tom this was a very emotional experience and one which thousands of other people appeared to share.

Pius was tall and thin, with a Roman nose and dark eyes behind gold-rimmed spectacles. He looked frail but in fact he had an enormous capacity for hard work. He was a remote figure and the general public saw him only rarely. Seminarians, though, had an advantage and were able to attend the ceremonies of beatification and canonisation in the Vatican Basilica.

Together with his fellow students, Tom also attended a number of papal audiences. Pius often addressed the audiences on complicated scientific and technological subjects in which he appeared to revel. When he addressed individuals, however, he was far from being the remote, ascetic intellectual. Rather, he was kindly. When he spoke to Tom he made him feel as if he was the only one in the room who mattered.

After the successful completion of his studies, Tom was awarded a Licentiate in Theology and the date of his ordination was set for December 18th, 1948. He was twenty-three, a year younger than the specified age for ordination. His superiors managed to obtain special permission for the ceremony to go ahead and it was decided that both he and Hugh McEwan should be made priests in the Basilica of St John Lateran, the Pope's Cathedral.

Throughout the years of preparation, Tom never had any serious doubts about his vocation, but like all candidates for the priesthood, he was given a final opportunity to reflect upon this most important decision in his life, on a pre-ordination retreat in the Jesuit Curia House. Hugh McEwan went with him.

It was during his stay in the mother house of the Society of Jesus that Tom became acutely aware that his was still very much a 'missionary' church. One room separated Tom's from Hugh's and the occupant seemed to spend most of his time typing. When he went out, he always locked his door. That was most unusual: surely your possessions could not have been in a safer place – in a house full of priests?

One day, the two students met this man in the corridor and recognised him immediately as Father Mochsi, a former scripture professor at the Gregorian University. He told them that he had returned to his native Hungary during the summer and now he had to go back again the following week. 'Pray for me,' he said, 'I'll probably be arrested when I get there!'

The week after Tom's ordination, Cardinal Jozsef Mindszenty, Primate of Hungary, was arrested and charged with treason by the communist government in Budapest. The Cardinal had refused to permit the Catholic schools of Hungary to be secularised. Tom wondered about his scripture professor. About a month later, there was a small item in *The Universe* indicating that he was to spend a number of years in a concentration camp. When Tom had seen him in the Jesuit house he had been drafting his report on the state of affairs in Hungary in his capacity as a Vatican Emissary.

The chance meeting with Father Mochsi greatly affected Tom. He admired the Jesuit's courage in returning to a country where Catholics were being persecuted and was determined that, when he went home to Scotland, he would never take his faith or the freedom to practise it, hard-won by previous generations, for granted.

December 18th, 1948: Ordination Day!
For the first time since coming to Rome, Tom met his mother and father, his sister Margaret and his uncles and aunts outside St John Lateran, before the big event. His father had closed the small confectionery business down, sold the machinery and used the proceeds to enable the family to be present at the ceremony. All the money went in one grand gesture!

Donny Renfrew was most anxious to attend the proceedings. However, there was a strange custom. It was forbidden to miss lectures at the Gregorian to attend a friend's ordination, unless you were assisting him in some way. There was nothing else for it but to play truant. So Donny and some others made their way to the Lateran to see Tom and Hugh.

Thirty-nine students from all over the world became priests on that particular day. The ceremonies started at 6.30 a.m., and the students' pre-communion fast had begun at midnight. When it was all over, Tom and Hugh returned to the Scots College to tell the Rector that they had been ordained. It was part of the custom that none of the college staff attended their students' ordinations either.

The Rector then knelt before the two new priests and asked for their blessing. At last the boys were allowed to go for breakfast, at a quarter to two in the afternoon.

There was another custom at that time for newly ordained priests to go along to Vatican Radio and broadcast their blessing to family, friends and neighbours in their home country. Tom and Hugh enjoyed this and a couple of days later, they had an audience with Pope Pius XII. He offered each of them his congratulations and blessings and spoke to their families.

Tom's superiors told him that he would be returning home to Scotland only for one year. The Glasgow archdiocese had recently been split into three and the new dioceses of Motherwell and Paisley had been formed. Tom's birthplace was Wishaw, so he was designated a Motherwell priest. He was appointed as an assistant in a small Parish in Lanarkshire: St Aloysius, Chapelhall. The Vicar General of Motherwell diocese confirmed that Tom would be going back to Rome in 1950 to study canon law, but meantime his days as a student were over.

CHAPTER THREE

Curate and Postgraduate

'Good morning, Father,' said the elderly man. 'Good morning, Father,' said his elderly wife. Tom Winning, the young, the very new priest, glanced quickly over his shoulder. Perhaps they were speaking to someone else? No – they were speaking to him.

'God bless you,' he said and they nodded and smiled. He was twenty-three and the couple, members of the parish to which he had been assigned in 1949, could well have been fifty years older. To them he was 'Father'. Tom had not really thought about this before, there was a sense of unreality. It was strange to him that the old folk did not find the situation slightly comical, as he did, but at the same time he was conscious of the respect and affection that the people of St Aloysius had for their priests. The parish was located in Chapelhall, near Airdrie. It had eight hundred parishioners.

The parish priest of St Aloysius, Peter Murie, a man in his sixties, always seemed to be on the brink of some severe illness. He had been advised by Monsignor Gerry Rogers, vicar general of Motherwell diocese, that the new curate, Father Winning, was well able to run the parish and after Tom had been there for a week, the senior man departed for a month's holiday, leaving Tom on his own.

The new curate was in his element and plunged into work. He felt he had received adequate training in Rome to equip him to deal with most sets of circumstances. However he did panic when he got his first two or three 'sick calls'. He had no experience of seeing a person dead or even terminally ill. It was a struggle to keep calm, to find words of comfort, to keep his hands from shaking when administering the Last Sacraments; and he found it was not something to which he became hardened.

To get things moving in the parish, Tom started up the Union of Catholic Mothers, a Young Men's Society and a Youth Club. Soon things were going with a swing and Tom began to enjoy himself thoroughly. In some ways though, he was very naïve and he learned a few hard lessons. He was startled that some of the parish members, the nicest, the kindest of people, would miss Mass on Sunday and not appear to be the least bit bothered by it. His experience had been that all Catholics went to Mass on Sunday.

He really did begin to re-examine his outlook when, after making a special plea from the pulpit to attract more people to the Holy Hour of Prayer on a Sunday night, not one extra soul turned up!

Tom's health improved with the better diet in Chapelhall and the duodenal ulcer which had bothered him so much prior to and during his time in Scots College seemed to give him less pain.

The parish priest had no complaints to make about his curate and when the time came for Tom to depart, to leave for Rome for the second time, Father Murie told Tom that it had been the easiest year he had ever had in his life.

Tom was on his way back to Rome to study church law, to learn all the regulations concerning things like the sacraments, religious vows, marriage cases and ecclesiastical burial. Monsignor Gerry Rogers, the vicar general in Motherwell, knew that in order to administer the diocese effectively, he would require priests with a thorough knowledge of the rules governing the internal life of the church. He was a canon lawyer himself and thought that Father Tom Winning would be able to cope very well with this type of work.

Tom was quite happy with the idea. He was to have a new companion on this second visit to Rome, Father John McQuade, born and educated in Ireland and with a reputation for having been a very bright student at St Patrick's College in Carlow. John was a priest in Motherwell diocese too but because he was Irish he was given a choice of pursuing his canon law studies in either Rome or Maynooth. He thought there was not much sense in having two canon lawyers in the diocese who had trained in different places, so he opted to go to Rome.

The two young priests were introduced to one another in Chapelhall by John's cousin, Jim McQuade, and they hit it off right away. However, Tom started to worry when he discovered that John had already taken classes in canon law, whereas he knew nothing about the subject. He had bought a copy of the *Coda* in Mill Hill but never found time to open it. Canon law was indeed a closed book to him!

Their next meeting was on the train to Rome. On the journey they met up with some other priests on their way to the Eternal City. These included Father O'Reilly – on course for a doctorate as Tom and John were – they hoped. Tom asked Father O'Reilly what he had been doing up until then. 'I've been teaching canon law for the past twelve years,' he said.

With the thought of all this competition, Tom spent the rest of the journey in a state of high anxiety. When studying for the licentiate, he had taken every advantage of dispensations from various subjects. He was beginning to regret the fact that he had never had a single class in canon law. Fortunately, Father O'Reilly turned out to be an unassuming type who did not need to impress anyone with his professional knowledge.

The door of the Scots College was opened to the arriving party of post-graduates by a young man in short trousers – Donny Renfrew – and he showed them to their rooms. Accustomed to the strict regime at Carlow, John was rather surprised by Donny's attire but he was soon to learn that, on account of the heat, it was the custom for students to wear shorts, putting on a soutane when they were going out.

To Tom, everything at the college was familiar but for John it was a novel experience. Having trained in a seminary holding one hundred and forty students he found the Scots College very small, as its number of students and staff never rose much above forty. In Carlow, students had not been allowed to speak to their professors. On his first day there, John had met the old Rector and engaged him in a long talk about apple growing, only to find out later that this was not the done thing. He was amazed to find that, in Rome, students were permitted to talk to the staff socially.

However, there was no special treatment for Tom and John, even though they were priests. They were both studying but they were not students. They felt as if they were living in a kind of no man's land, having to conform, more or less, to the rules that governed the seminarians. They grew to feel that nobody was really interested in them and became engrossed in their studies.

Hugh McEwan, who had been working as a priest in Glasgow Archdiocese, came back to Rome too, both to study for a doctorate in theology and take up a post as a member of the college staff. At mealtimes, Hugh ate at the Rector's table while Tom and John were required to sit with the students. Some post-graduates resented this division of 'them' and 'us' but Tom and John soon became so involved in canon law that they had no time to let the hierarchical structure of college life affect them.

The canon law lectures were conducted, in Latin, at the Gregorian University. John found it difficult to follow the Latin at first and it took him about three months to become attuned. Tom's Latin was fluent so he could concentrate on learning the law. Soon they were on good terms with the English-speaking scholars in their class and they became friends with an American, Father Paul Marcinkus, known as 'Cink', who came from Chicago.

The canon law course took three years to complete: two years' study and another to write a thesis. Tom thought his teachers were quite outstanding. One impressed him in particular: Padre Cappello, a tiny, saintly, old man, reminiscent of a sparrow. However, he did not make his piety obvious through his lectures. He would simply come into the auditorium with no notes at all and rattle off the canons. This was no mean feat as there were about two thousand, three hundred of them.

Tom discovered that this diminutive genius had a very interesting history. He started off as a priest in North Italy, moving to one of the seminaries to lecture in canon law and moral theology. Around this time, the beginning of the century, the movement known as Modernism was causing anxiety in the church, especially during the pontificate of Pius x. The Modernists were a group of priests who attempted to make Catholicism more palatable to the thought of the day. They said that Catholicism did not have an objective supernatural character and reduced it to a matter of individual religious psychology. The Modernists were never very numerous but they did occupy important positions in a number of seminaries and universities and the fear was that their philosophy would gradually corrupt the faith of the clergy and lay people whom they taught. A kind of witch hunt developed, mainly in Italy, leading to a number of priests being taken out of seminary training, including Padre Cappello, although he was completely orthodox.

Cappello came to Rome to lecture in a minor subject at the Lateran University and there he decided to become a Jesuit. When he joined the ranks of the Society of Jesus his fortunes changed. Pope

Pius x – the man who had removed Cappello from his position in the seminary – had written a decree in 1905 on how often Catholics should receive communion. Cappello wrote a commentary on the Pope's decree and soon he was given a job as Lecturer in Canon Law at the Gregorian University. There he taught for many years and became known as one of the real experts in the subject. He was a consultant to practically every congregation in Rome, the big committees which deal with all major matters in the church.

When he finished his lectures, Cappello would go down to the Church of St Ignatius and hear confessions for five or six hours. After Cappello's death, his body lay in state in the University Chapel, and for three or four days, thousands of Italians filed past to pay their respects to him. He was a humble little man who did not draw attention to himself. Nevertheless, much was written about him and he was so well-known for his personal holiness that preliminary steps were taken to have him canonised.

Tom had been astonished by Cappello's prodigious memory. It was a herculean task, learning the church laws, and during his first year, Tom worked and worked, like a Trojan, so much so that, when the time came for the first year final examinations in June 1951, he could hardly walk. He had to take a taxi to the examination hall and afterwards went straight to bed, where he had to stay for about ten days with what seemed to be some terrible form of rheumatism.

Unlike the student priests, postgraduates were allowed home for the summer vacation. Tom had arranged to go to Lourdes, the famous pilgrimage centre in the South of France, on his way back to Scotland. For nearly a hundred years thousands of spiritually and physically sick people had drunk the water at Lourdes and bathed in it, hoping to be healed. The doctor in Rome whom Tom had consulted about his aching limbs was an atheist and had no belief in the reputedly curative effect of Lourdes water. He warned Tom not to go into the baths at the Lourdes Grotto. Tom did as he was told.

When he arrived back in Scotland, he attended a clinic where a physiotherapist informed him that there were nodules on all his joints, brought about by rheumatoid arthritis. 'It's bad!' he told him, but after twelve treatments in a month, the trouble disappeared, never to return.

It appeared that Tom over-extended himself in the first year but the second year of the course was fine and he paced himself better. There was some friendly rivalry among the members of the canon law class. Two Capuchins, members of the Franciscan Order who are bound by vows of poverty, always sat in front of Tom and John at lectures. The latter were amazed that these friars regularly seemed to be wearing new soutanes.

For Tom and John one of the main problems was lack of money. They had about £40 a year as pay and whatever they could pick up as Mass stipends – the equivalent of twenty five pence a time, with a maximum of seven in any one week in Rome. They had to buy stacks of books using their own money but could not afford to get more than half of those recommended by the professors.

'Buy this book! Buy that book!' they were told on Monday, and on Tuesday the Capuchins were in the lecture theatre with the book or books mentioned. Tom discovered that it was the friars' Religious Superior who was looking after their needs and John observed wryly that those in religious orders took the vow of poverty but it was ordinary priests who had to practise it!

During termtime, Tom and John enjoyed short breaks and visited Anzio, Florence and Assisi. On one occasion they went to Lake Como. There they found a lovely little church and were intrigued to learn that, since the Reformation, five long-lived parish priests had been enough to keep the parish running continuously. In the past, parish priests were never switched about – it was a lifelong appointment.

On their travels around Italy, Tom always did the talking as his knowledge of the language was good. John was quite embarrassed by his failure to grasp Italian. One day, he went to a paper-stall and asked for an *Espresso*. thinking he would get a *Daily Express*. It caused so much amusement that he was put off trying to speak Italian for the future. Actually, they both drank quite a lot of espressos to keep themselves awake in the afternoons and for a boost before exams.

The fact that Tom knew where to find the cheap restaurants was useful for, although the meals at college were better than they had been during his first stay in Rome, they were not particularly large. John accepted the meagre fare with his customary humour, telling Tom it was a well-known fact that, should any church official, priest or archbishop, be found overpaying or overfeeding anyone, he would go to purgatory for many, many years!

John's banter and easygoing manner helped to make the rigours of the canon law course more bearable and when it came to the third and final year, Tom found himself really enjoying his studies. His thesis topic was *Tithes in Scotland* and in effect it became more of a historical project than a religious one. During the summer vacations when he had gone back home, he spent a lot of time in the Baillie Institute in Glasgow, studying charters and documents relating to Scottish abbeys. When he returned to Rome, he was still able to borrow papers from any library in Scotland, paying only the postage to and from Italy, a facility which he and many other fellow students greatly appreciated.

The final doctorate examination involved lecturing in Latin before four or five professors on a subject chosen by them, for a period of forty-five minutes. The students were given only an overnight warning of what was to come. It was a nerve wracking experience but both Tom and John passed *cum laude.*

This time there was no formal graduation ceremony. Tom, now Doctor Winning, was told that he would be leaving Rome to take up a post as curate at St Mary's Church in Hamilton. Doctor John McQuade was assigned to St John's, Uddingston. Their canon law qualifications were going to be put to use in dealing with appeals for marriage annulments in Motherwell diocese.

Tom had not been home since the summer vacation of 1952 and on his return was shocked to find that his mother was ill and had not been well for nearly a year. The family had decided not to tell him, in case it upset his ability to concentrate on his studies. Although she had her own doctor, Tom took her to see a specialist in Glasgow. All he could tell Tom was that his mother's condition was hopeless, her tumour was incurable. She was admitted to the Royal Infirmary and her life expectancy was put at three weeks. In fact, she lingered on for ten months and died in September 1954. It was a big upset.

During this period, Tom also had to settle into his new post. The man in charge of St Mary's – Father Hamilton – had been a priest in St Patrick's so he already knew Tom quite well. There were two other curates.

Father Hamilton was a man with high standards of church life – one of few at that time who would encourage serious discussion at table on theology or any branch of church affairs. However, he did not do a great deal of parish work himself, leaving most of it to the curates.

Father Hamilton always held himself aloof. He could never make friends and Tom put this down to the fact that he had lost his mother at an early age and had been starved of affection. On one or two occasions he unbent a little and it seemed that there could be a real person inside him straining to get out, but his personality was fixed and unchangeable. He told other colleagues that he thought highly of his new curate but he was unable to tell Tom this fact to his face.

One of the curates, Father John Boyle, was about Tom's own age while the other, Father John Murray, seemed comparatively elderly. Father Murray was most anxious to get a parish of his own and constantly looked forward to the time when he would be in charge. Eventually, he was given the task of setting up the parish of St Mungo's in Garthamlock. Unfortunately, his health broke down and he got little opportunity to enjoy the realisation of his ambitions.

Working with Fathers Hamilton and Murray, Tom Winning learned that for some men the priestly life could be both lonely and frustrating at times. Although Tom knew that having a canon law degree was a step in the right direction for the promotion-conscious, he was content at that stage of his life simply to remain a curate. He was convinced that his poor health record would preclude him from any advancement anyway, for as a result of his illness in Rome, Tom was more or less regarded as being 'delicate'. On his return to the Scots College for postgraduate study, the Spiritual Director, Father Denis Meechan, had told him: 'I was sure that you were never going to see your ordination. I thought you were going to die!' So, unlike the hapless Father Murray, Father Tom Winning had no ambitions at this time.

When Tom was working in St Mary's, the first Bishop of Motherwell, Edward Douglas, retired and was replaced by Bishop James Donald Scanlan, transferred from the diocese of Dunkeld. Scanlan took over the premises occupied by Monsignor Rogers, the vicar general, and Rogers came to stay with the priests in St Mary's for a while.

Tom found Gerry Rogers to be a kindred spirit. He did not know it then, of course, but the kindly Monsignor was to be one of the most significant influences on his career in the church. They had first met back in 1946, when Monsignor Rogers had been one of the party waiting to welcome the boys to the Scots College on its re-opening after the war. It was he who had sent Tom and John McQuade to Rome to study canon law. He was the decision-maker in the diocese of Motherwell, always striding about, getting things done. Tom felt he brought a new vitality to St Mary's.

Gerry Rogers came from Dennistoun in Glasgow and, like Tom, had studied at the Gregorian University. He too had been enthralled by Rome. The Eternal City had cast its spell over him with a more than usual share of that special 'aura' which in those days seemed, to Catholics at least, to be given to those priests who spent their formative years there. In the thirties, Gerry worked as an assistant priest in St John's, Portugal Street, in Glasgow. Recognising his great potential, Archbishop Donald MacIntosh had encouraged him to return to Rome to take a degree in canon law. Thereafter, he worked closely with MacIntosh, and became President of the Archdiocesan Marriage Tribunal. When the new Motherwell diocese was set up in 1948, Gerry happened to be resident in Lanarkshire and automatically became a priest of Motherwell. Bishop Douglas appointed him his right hand man and when Bishop Scanlan succeeded Douglas, Gerry, by then Monsignor Rogers, continued as vicar general.

Gerry was a tall, handsome man, genial and good-natured. Bing Crosby might well have based his film character of Father O'Malley on him. He had great organisational ability and a great facility for dealing with problems in a very short time. Those who did not have his talent claimed he was work-shy but the truth was that he could deal in half an hour with jobs that most people would require three hours to complete. When he was appointed vicar general he went to Glasgow University and took a civil law degree to help him with his work in the Motherwell Marriage Tribunal. He still managed to find time to play golf, which was his great hobby.

Tom Winning was sorry when Monsignor Rogers was transferred to Motherwell Cathedral as administrator but he was not to miss him for long. Bishop Scanlan appointed Tom diocesan secretary and he was required to move to the cathedral too, in 1957. Had the Monsignor put in a good word for the 'sickly' curate? His stay at the cathedral, however, was short-lived. Exactly one year after his transfer, Bishop Scanlan sent for Tom and told him that he was to go to the

Franciscan Convent in Bothwell as chaplain, whilst continuing his work as diocesan secretary. Tom was required to move his goods and chattels to a little three-roomed house. He was unused to living alone and missed the company and cheery atmosphere of the cathedral.

Tom's first day as chaplain was 3 October, 1958 – the Feast of St Theresa – and his first task was to say early morning Mass for the sisters. He was scheduled to drive the bishop to the opening of the new St Theresa's Church in Galloway diocese, so decided to conduct the ceremony of Benediction immediately after Mass as he would not be available at four o'clock, the customary time for this liturgical service. During Benediction, the priest is required to put a vestment around his shoulders known as a cope, often fairly heavy and richly embroidered. After he concluded his first Mass as chaplain, Tom started the Benediction and put on the cope. He noticed that the threads were giving way on the hooks of the vestment and feeling it would slide off his shoulders, he took it off and threw it over the altar-rails.

Tom had had no time to get acquainted with the nuns so he was unaware that one of their number, a redoubtable old lady, was legendary because of her ability to open her mouth and put her foot in it. Having observed Tom's pale face, his ascetically thin frame and the fact that he had removed the cope before the Benediction was over, Sister Elizabeth O'Connell was in no doubt. 'Oh God!' she said, in an audible voice, 'They've sent us another sick priest!' The rest of the community had great difficulty in stifling their mirth and Tom knew his job as chaplain would be no sinecure.

As well as having responsibility for the sisters' spiritual welfare, he said Mass for the pupils who attended their private school, worked at the Marriage Tribunal with Gerry Rogers and John McQuade, and carried out his duties as Diocesan Secretary. He liked being at the hub of things and now he was working for a most unusual character:

James Donald Scanlan, Bishop of Motherwell, a colourful personality if ever there was one.

CHAPTER FOUR

The Bishop's Secretary

Tom had heard of 'JD' as he was known, long before he was appointed to work as his secretary. He knew that the bishop liked to affect a grand manner in public but soon discovered that he was something of a paradox, because his personal life was remarkably simple. Born in Glasgow in 1899, Bishop Scanlan never lost the aura of the Edwardian era during which he was brought up.

The bishop had a number of idiosyncrasies. One which his clergy found most puzzling was the fact that he would not permit church business to be discussed when he was at the dinner table with his priests. Anyone who unwittingly raised some problem of a pastoral or spiritual nature was simply ignored.

Bishop Scanlan encouraged the formation of troops of Boy Scouts, partly because he enjoyed taking the salute at their parades. He asked Tom Winning to build up the scouts. This was somewhat ironic as Tom knew nothing about scouts and used to laugh at Donny Renfrew and make jokes about the scout movement for which Donny had a lot of enthusiasm. Obediently, Tom recruited about thirty Scouts in St Mary's, rigged them all out and had parade in full uniform, not realising that he should not have done that until they had passed certain elementary tests.

Working with the bishop, Tom Winning soon realised that he expected efficiency from his subordinates. When it came to correspondence leaving the diocesan office, Scanlan was pernickety to a fault. No matter what Tom wrote, he would make a point of changing it in some way. Every morning he would read the incoming mail aloud. This was good experience for Tom, as he got to know about diocesan business and how to deal with it. Bishop Scanlan himself was a voluminous letter writer to all sorts of people not just in Scotland but across Europe.

Tom found his new 'boss' could be explosive on occasion. 'That's so and so on the phone for you,' Tom would say to him. 'Tell him I'll blow his brains out!' Scanlan would shout, if the caller had in some way not come up to his expectations. A pressman once heard what Scanlan was shouting before Tom remembered to cover the mouthpiece of the phone. 'Oh well, that's that then!' said the journalist and hung up.

Priests with problems felt nervous when they had to have an interview with their bishop, but, provided they had made a formal written appointment to see him, they invariably found him sympathetic.

Bishop Scanlan's greatest delight was to get dressed up in complete episcopal regalia and, with the help of a well-drilled master of ceremonies, bring the full ceremonial of the church into various parishes of the diocese. Not one of the smallest details was to be overlooked. When he called on the civic authorities, his attire was fit for some great Vatican occasion. He often used to say that the smaller the town, the more self-important the provost, so it was important to recognise that. As he got to know Bishop Scanlan, Tom realised that he was obviously ambitious in terms of personal prestige but not for any other kind of gain. The bishop had a deep sense of making the church present in public life through his becoming involved in the civic life of the community. He believed that by becoming a well-known figure in Lanarkshire and beyond, he was putting the Catholic Church 'on the map' in Scotland.

Bishop Scanlan had a reputation as a great raconteur with a taste for history rather than theology. He had a fund of stories to tell, drawing upon his life experiences before he became a bishop. In many ways he was not on the same wavelength as his fellow clergymen who had gone from school to the seminary, to the university and then to the parish. His background was quite different from theirs. Indeed, that he became a priest at all seemed extraordinary.

James Scanlan's father, an affluent doctor with a successful practice in Calton, in Glasgow's East End, was disappointed when his son expressed the desire to become a priest. Doctor Scanlan was a confirmed anti-cleric. He had ensured that his son had been well educated at St Mungo's Academy and St Aloysius College. In 1916, James had entered the Royal Military College, Sandhurst, in the middle of World War I and the following year, at the age of eighteen, was commissioned second lieutenant and posted to Egypt to join a Glasgow regiment, the Highland Light Infantry. The long-standing tradition in the British Army that no-one talks 'shop' at dinner or in the Officers' Mess would have been a lesson Scanlan would have learned at Sandhurst and which might have explained his later reluctance to discuss diocesan problems when dining with his priests. After War service, he studied law at Glasgow University – one of a very small minority of Catholic students in the university at that time – and, on graduating, it seemed as if a good career lay ahead of him. He decided, however, to be a 'career' priest and applied to enter St Edward's College, Ware, rather than any of the Scottish seminaries. He was or-dained at Westminster Cathedral and continued his studies at the Institute Catholique in Paris and the Appollinare in Rome (the 'Sandhurst' of the Holy See), where he graduated as a canon lawyer. During the thirties he worked at the Westminster Marriage Tribunal, dealing with the marital problems of the upper classes, the better-off Catholics, not just from London but from other areas. By 1945, he was a Monsignor and Chancellor of the Diocese of Westminster.

Despite the fact that he had chosen to be a priest of Westminster rather than Glasgow, he seemed proud of his roots and was well-known for his helpfulness to fellow Scots when they visited London and great hospitality to the college staff of St Peter's when they moved to Mill Hill. He returned north when the Apostolic Delegate, Archbishop Godfrey of Westminster, nominated him to be 'co-adjutor' – assistant bishop with right of succession – to help the ninety-year-old Bishop Toner of Dunkeld diocese.

To say that his appointment caused a stir in the church in the Dundee area is to understate the case. James Scanlan's name had never been included among those thought by the Scottish hierarchy to be suitable candidates for the role of bishop – their *episcopabile* list. What would this Monsignor Scanlan know of the problems of Scottish Catholics in poor, working-class areas? His background and lifestyle were entirely different from those of the clergy of Dunkeld. How would he be able to relate to them?

After seventeen years as a priest, James Scanlan now had an op-portunity to see how the other half lived – the ordinary, overworked priests of a poor diocese. He was unable to help with more priests, who were in short supply, but with his connections down south, he was able to bring in members of religious orders to assist with day-today problems. He maintained his own style, succeeding in bringing a different perspective to the diocese where he remained for nine years, before going to Motherwell.

Scanlan was a shrewd man. He saw that he had a first class administrator in Gerry Rogers and, although they were quite different from one another, the two men made an effective team. Rogers was put in charge of the organisation and policy-making in the diocese, while the bishop was the front-runner, the man in the middle of the stage, concerned mainly with projecting an image of the church as confident and healthy.

Indeed it seemed as if Bishop Scanlan's real work for the advancement of the church in Scotland was getting under way. New churches were being built, new parishes founded. Some said that James Scanlan used the church for his own ends, for self-aggrandisement and certainly he revelled in the role of bishop. Yet there was no doubt that his main aim was to tell the Catholic community that it had nothing about which to feel inferior. By fostering good relations with the civic authorities he showed that the world outside the church was important too.

These were lessons which Tom Winning was absorbing during the time he worked for the bishop, without being overly conscious of it. He was filing away other things in his mind too, sometimes even saying to himself: 'Well, I wouldn't do it that way, if I got the chance!'

He was too far down the pecking order to offer any opinions to his superior – not that he would have dared even if he had been given the opportunity. Tom did not dislike Bishop Scanlan, though like most young curates he was very much in awe of him. Scanlan had the manners of an Edwardian gentleman and was given neither to emotion nor affection in his relations with others. In the diocesan office he maintained an air of formality, greeting Monsignor Rogers every day with a hearty: 'Good morning, Vicar!' and always calling Tom, 'Doctor Winning'. His young secretary could not have been more different. Born and brought up in Lanarkshire, Tom had never been one to stand on ceremony. He was, by nature, forthright, in fact some thought he could be on occasion rather too blunt. His life had been insular in comparison to the bishop's and at first he was unsure how to respond to him. Their relationship grew into one based on mutual respect rather than friendship. Tom Winning was an apparently indefatigable worker who seldom took a day off and Bishop Scanlan, always punctilious about his own devotions and appointments, could not fail to appreciate this.

In 1959, Bishop Scanlan nominated Tom's friend, Monsignor Rogers, to a top job in Rome, as a judge in the church's supreme court of appeal for marriage cases, known as the *Rota*. Rogers was to succeed a friend of the bishop's and a fellow Scot, Monsignor Heard, who had become a cardinal. The people of Motherwell diocese were sorry to see the popular Monsignor go – many said he would surely be made a bishop before long.

The Rota had about a dozen judges – rather similar to the Court of Session judges in Scotland. They were appointed because they were considered to be brilliant men, among the best jurists in the world. For Gerry Rogers, at fifty-two, and after many years of practical work, the return to books and study would involve a real effort, but no-one who knew him had any doubt that his natural flair and commitment would ensure his success in the post.

For Tom, too, the end of the decade brought changes, both in his personal and working life. His father, after having a bout of flu from which he seemed to recover, died quite suddenly of a cerebral haemorrhage. Now both his parents were dead: life would never be the same again.

Tom's sister Margaret had married Eddie McCarron four years before. He remained close to her and developed a great affection for her two children, Agnes, born in 1956 and Edward, two years her junior. Tom did not socialise much and when he did take a break, which was rare, he always went to his sister's home.

His propensity to overwork, combined with the shock of his father's death, proved to be an intolerable strain on his health. The ulcer which he had had for sixteen years flared up again and in 1960 he had a haemorrhage. He was given little time to recover when, the following year, he was informed of another change of appointment. Now he was to take up the post of Spiritual Director at the Scots College. The Rector, Monsignor Flanagan, had requested that Tom be given the position and did not seem to be concerned about his health problems. Bishop Scanlan appeared to concur with Flanagan on this; indeed the only condition which he laid down for Tom's release from Motherwell diocese was one which would help him on

his career path and bore no relation to his illness. Scanlan stated that
Tom should continue his canon law studies, this time at the Rota. He
felt that this would provide a second interest for him and would not
encroach too much on his work with the students. Moreover, at the
Rota he could renew his acquaintance with his 'friend at court',
Monsignor Rogers.

Tom was on his way back to Rome again.

CHAPTER FIVE

The Spiritual Director

After he had been told of his new appointment, Tom was given two weeks to move. He had been working in Lanarkshire for nine years, at the very centre of diocesan activities and, much as he loved Rome, the prospect of being confined to the college again was a daunting one. His superiors had a higher opinion of him than he had of himself – he did not think he was good enough to take up the responsible position of Spiritual Director and his nervous anticipation exacerbated his health problems. By the time he left for Rome he was totally exhausted and when he got there he had to go straight to bed. In December he was admitted to the Calvary Hospital to have his ulcer removed and it was 20 February of the following year before he was fit enough to give his first talk to the students.

Tom found that, as Spiritual Director, he occupied a unique position on the staff. He had nothing to do with the discipline, academic work or running of the college. His responsibility was to prepare students for the priesthood from a strictly spiritual point of view. He was required to speak to them about different aspects of the church, the Christian life, their future as priests and the various responsibilities they would be required to undertake. He was always to be available to give counselling, leading the students towards some kind of stable spiritual approach to their lives and work, discussing their relationship with God. As Spiritual Director he was endowed with an independence from other aspects of college life since most of his information about students was gained in confidence, in the confessional.

Despite initial uncertainty regarding his suitability for the job, he settled into it much more effectively than he had ever dreamed. He had the opportunity to help young men attain priesthood and, in a sense, to reorder the spiritual direction in the college to meet some of the requirements he had as a young student himself and which he felt had not always been satisfied. In the past the role of Spiritual Director had been a passive one – it was left up to the students to seek him out for advice. Father Tom Winning was anxious to make it an active role and wanted a strong element of 'formation' in the college's spiritual programme.

His main preoccupation was to make it as easy as possible for men to know how to pray and how to mature spiritually. He soon realised the benefit of being taken away from the fast-moving life of a priest in the diocese to a quieter, almost contemplative existence. After nine years he was being given an opportunity to recharge his batteries, take a look at what was happening in the church in general, get down to some serious reading and, at the same time attend four classes per month at the Rota. He often thought that being Spiritual Director probably did more for him as a person than he was able to do for the students. He felt it was just not possible to go on encouraging men to give of their best without some spiritual benefit accruing to himself.

The students at Scots College liked his style. His natural informality was completely refreshing because it was in such sharp contrast to the rest of the staff at the time and to the previous Director, Monsignor Matthew Kinsella. He had something in common with Mat Kinsella, however, for both of them had been born and brought up within a mile of each other. Even more coincidentally, Kinsella's predecessor hailed from the same area of Wishaw too and Tom's successor was also to come from St Patrick's, Shieldmuir.

Tom Winning was closer to the students in age than Monsignor Kinsella and he seemed to understand them. He maintained a friendly, relaxed manner and the seminarians appreciated his directness and his dislike of humbug of any kind, at any time, in anybody. His health improved again but he was still totally work-oriented, and during his five-year stay in Rome he played one game of golf and went to one football match. After a while, being confined to the same building both during the day and in the evenings became rather trying. The only outsider with whom Tom was friendly was a layman on the Rota course, and after the course was completed, he officiated at his wedding. Apart from that, he was cocooned in a strictly ecclesiastical atmosphere.

Tom found the Rota studies a welcome diversion though the examination process he had to go through was the toughest in the church. In a three-year period there were only four classes a month but, overall, it was a time of high-powered concentrated research.

Marks were awarded on monthly exams, each of which consisted of a problem – a marriage case or a case of ecclesiastical discipline which the student had never come across before. This was to be researched and findings put forward in writing within the month. At the end of the year, there was a three-hour written exam which could be described as reasonable if all the work had been done.

The sting in the tail was the final examination at the end of the three years: a twelve-hour written paper from 9.00 a.m to 9.00 p.m. No breaks for meals. Bring your own food and drink – in Tom's case, banana sandwiches and a flask of coffee. It was held on 5 July, so hot that Tom wondered if Rome was burning again. The examination itself, which was in Latin, was to read a whole marriage case and then write the judges' sentence on it. The evidence of witnesses which was in French, Italian and Latin, had to be translated. It was anything but straightforward, a very tricky case. Six sat the exam that year. There was one failure – known as the 'Flying Spaniard' – because he travelled every month by plane from Madrid to Rome for Rota lectures. Two members of the class withdrew at the last minute, both native Romans.

By passing the examinations, Tom Winning now had the title 'Advocate of the Sacred Roman Rota' which would entitle him to plead for Catholic people, who wished to have their marriages annulled, at the church's highest 'court'. He gained valuable experience through his friendship with Monsignor Rogers, who was now an established judge at the Rota. He gave Tom the opportunity to work as a Notary, taking evidence, in a number of marriage cases of English-speaking couples, including the case of Lee Radziwill, Jackie Kennedy's sister. Tom enjoyed this work although his job as Spiritual Director remained his priority.

The Scots College students and staff experienced some upheaval in their lives with the sale of their seminary building in 1962. Radical reconstruction was required to repair the damage done to its fabric during the war and it was considered that the cost of restoration would be excessive in proportion to the effect. Re-building on the site was not permitted by the city authorities and so the Scottish bishops decided to rebuild the college on the outskirts of Rome on the Via Cassia. During the two years' interval between the sale of the old college and the completion of the new, the whole community stayed at the villa in Marino. Each day the students travelled by bus into the city centre for their classes at the university, a long journey. Father Tom Winning and two colleagues on the staff, Fathers Hugh McEwan and James Foley, had equal shares in a small cinquecento car to take them around.

1962 also saw the start of a major upheaval in the Catholic Church itself. Since Tom had last been in Rome, Pius xii had died and Angelo Roncalli, the Patriarch of Venice, had been voted by his fellow cardinals to succeed him, as Pope John xxiii. He was nearly seventy-seven years old when elected in October 1958 and many be-lieved they had an 'interim' Pope who would maintain the status quo and make no drastic changes in the church. They thought that perhaps he would go as far as bringing the college of cardinals up to what was then considered full strength – seventy – from fifty-four. Then there would be more men to choose from at the next papal election. Pope John would serve as a bridge between one Pope, Pius xii, and another.

Those who held this view did not know Angelo Roncalli. He was no interim Pope. Three months after he took office, he announced that there was going to be an 'ecumenical council' in Rome – a gathering together of all cardinals, archbishops, bishops and heads of religious orders from the entire world. He had decided that the church needed a breath of fresh air to sweep through it. He wanted it to be renewed, geared to the needs of the twentieth century, revitalised for the future but remaining continuous with its ancient past; and he wanted the leaders of the church to discuss how these ideas could be put into effect. There had not been such a meeting since the First Vatican Council in 1869-70.

Pius xii had already brought about some changes in the church. He had introduced evening Masses, promoted the Latin dialogue Mass in which lay people made the responses aloud, and changed the rules regarding fasting and abstinence. Before receiving communion, Catholics had to fast from solid food and alcoholic drink from mid-night. The period of fast was cut to three hours in 1957. The rule about abstinence from fresh meat on a Friday, which had been sus-pended during the years of rationing, was beginning to lose some of its importance. Pius made it 'easier' for people to be Catholics but these changes paled into insignificance in comparison with those which came about as a result of John xxiii's Vatican Council ii. It was not a breath of air he let into the church, it was a whirlwind.

Thirty-five hundred bishops and heads of religious orders came to Rome in October 1962 for the first sessions. Some of them must have wondered why they had been invited. After all, Vatican Council I had produced a dogma stating that, when speaking *ex cathedra* in matters of faith and morals, the Pope was infallible. What more was there to be said? The Catholic Church already had all the answers. Vatican I had been adjourned when Rome fell to King Victor Emmanuel's troops, before the role of bishops in church could be clarified. So for years, bishops always did what 'Rome' said, 'Rome' being a succession of popes who ruled as absolute monarchs, together with their bureaucrats, the cardinals of the curia, each of whom headed the different Vatican departments. The curia wielded enormous power. It was this highly conservative body which dissuaded Pope Pius XII from calling a council himself and nearly succeeded in putting John XXIII off the idea too. However, John was determined that the council sessions should go ahead and, although subject to his authority, the whole procedure was to be democratic, each bishop being allowed to have his say if he wanted to do so. This was most un-usual and some must have wondered if such a thing were possible. A Vatican Preparatory Commission, organised by the curia, had sought the bishops' opinions regarding the topics and problems which should be discussed and their replies were published in fifteen bulging volumes, called the *Acta*. Thus it seemed as if many of the bishops thought that the church did indeed require a great renewal but in fact the expectations of the majority of the world's episcopate were narrow and limited.

The bishops of the Scottish hierarchy made their way to Rome with all the others but renewal in the church was not one of their priorities. Back home they had their hands full attempting to provide parishes and schools for the ever-burgeoning Catholic population and to keep down the numbers of those lapsing from the practice of their faith. Scottish Catholics were gradually beginning to lose the 'poor immigrant church' image and were now a powerful and respectable religious minority. The bishops did not want the barque of Peter to be rocked with any new-fangled ideas at this stage.

The only place large enough to accommodate Vatican II was the nave of St Peter's basilica. Observers from other churches had been invited and each participating bishop could bring up to four secretaries or advisers for consultation on theological or canonical matters. These advisers were known as *periti*. The Scottish and South Korean hierarchies were the only two groups which did not bring even one *peritus* with them. Perhaps the Scottish bishops thought that there was sufficient expertise among their own college staff if they needed specialised knowledge. The Rector, Phil Flanagan and Hugh McEwan, who had become Vice Rector, both had doctorates in theology. The Tutor or *Ripetitore,* James Foley, was a scripture scholar and Tom had his degree in canon law. When they came to Rome, Flanagan told the bishops what to expect from the council: he predicted that it would draw out the implications of papal 'infallibility' and involve discussion on the role of bishops *vis à vis* the Pope. There would be other items on the agenda, such as the reform of the liturgy, the role of the laity and the promotion of Christian unity – but he believed, as did many others, that the council, although officially designated Vatican ii, would be, in the main, a continuation of the council held in 1870.

It seemed the curia members felt this way too, that the bishops were in Rome to 'rubber stamp' their own decisions. On the very first day of council deliberations, they produced a tract they had already prepared on the theological nature of the church. They had also drawn up a list of names of bishops whom they recommended should be elected members of the ten permanent commissions of the council. It was assumed that all the bishops would accept these nominations without question. But an extraordinary thing happened: the bishops disagreed with the curia. Deciding to embrace the Pope's idea of democratic discussion whole-heartedly, a number of them said they wanted to choose commission members themselves, without limitations. The opening session was adjourned and the bishops given three days to consult and draw up their own lists. Their first meeting had lasted approximately half an hour, but in that short time, members of the hierarchies of France, Germany, Belgium, Holland and Spain, showed that they were not going to have council proceedings manipulated by the traditionalists in the curia. They were determined that Vatican ii was going to be a genuine attempt on the part of the church to engage in real, critical self-evaluation, not a mere routine acceptance of proposals and edicts made by the men at the top. Pope John was pleased with what had happened, but now the council was to continue in a direction which no-one had expected.

The Scottish bishops attended all the council meetings conscientiously but they were out of their depth compared to their continental colleagues. They were hampered by the use of Latin – the official language of the council – in the huge building of St Peter's, with poor acoustics and inadequate microphones. Often Bishop Hart of Dunkeld had to move out of his seat to hear what was going on when the discussions became a mere blur of sound. As well as that, their guiding light, Monsignor Flanagan, now knew no more than they did about what was going to happen. Archbishop Gray, as the senior bishop, wanted to speak at the council and drew up an 'intervention' with Flanagan's help. However, each time he put his name forward to speak, it coincided with the guillotine on the day's proceedings and his interventions were relegated to the *Acta* of the Council. The Scottish bishops experienced a crisis of confidence.

Tom Winning took an interest in what was going on in Vatican II but could become involved only peripherally. He never had an opportunity to attend even one session of the council. The Scots hierarchy was not too familiar with the Roman scene – Archbishop Campbell, the only one who had studied in Rome, died just after the council started. Not knowing the ropes, they were reluctant to ask for the privileges which would have enabled college staff members, including Tom, to attend even one morning session. Moreover, the Scottish bishops seemed to take the contract of secrecy regarding council sessions a good deal more seriously than other groups of bishops, so it was difficult in the early days of Vatican II to find out from them what was being discussed at St Peter's. Fortunately, it was a daily occurrence for theologians, the *periti* and other bishops to give talks in the different colleges on the topics being debated at the council. Some of the leading lights in the lecture circuit were Bishop Wright of Pittsburgh and the theologians Karl Rahner and Hans Küng. Tom Winning found it difficult to find time to attend many of these lectures but after he passed his Rota examination, the bishops invited him to be their canon law consultant when they had their own conferences at the Scots College and he became their Minute Secretary. Thus he was able to learn much more about what was going on. He appreciated this but the fact that he was allowed to sit in on meetings created a distinct 'atmosphere' between the Auxiliary Bishop of Glasgow, James Ward, and himself. Under the statutes of the Scottish Bishops' Conference at that time, Ward, as an auxiliary, was not allowed to attend the meetings. Why the bishops could not have waived the rule in this case seems odd, as Ward was attending all the sessions at St Peter's. The bishop would go for a walk when his colleagues and Tom were in conference. Ward could not be blamed for feeling unhappy about his exclusion. Unfortunately he directed his resentment towards Tom Winning who had no say in the matter. This situation was not to help their association in the future.

The Scots bishops never brought any ecclesiastically well-known figures back to lunch or supper at the college. They were more likely to bring back bishops from Australia, America or New Zealand to the college, people with whom they shared a common language. They did not seem to have any time to waste on socialising when they were in Rome. Nevertheless, they did make some contacts and this helped them to mature a great deal in their role as bishops. The Scots hierarchy was a modest, humble group of men, good pastors, but they were not theologians and found the sessions heavy going at times. Despite all their difficulties, they kept their sense of humour and attended St Peter's assiduously. Fathers Winning, McEwan and Foley used to drive them to the Vatican for meetings at 9.00 a.m. collecting them again at 12.30 p.m. Tom thought they were kindly men and was impressed by the fact that, even though some of them were reluctant to stay away from their dioceses for three or four months at a stretch, every year for four years, they did so with a good grace.

The Scots bishops were not alone in finding Vatican II a taxing experience. Those who had a 'traditional' view of the church – most of the Italians, many from the United States and other parts of the world – found themselves strongly opposing the 'liberals' from West Germany, France, Belgium, Holland and Spain. The curial cardinals felt most under threat. The first topic which was discussed concerned the Mass. Should it continue to be said in Latin or be translated into the language of each country? The debate itself was conducted in Latin, which had been used in church liturgy since the third century. Traditionalists wanted no change, saying that the use of Latin unified the church; they were opposed by those who believed that Catholics could participate more fully in the Mass if it was said in their own language.

Cardinal Alfredo Ottaviani, Secretary of the Sacred Supreme Congregation of the Holy Office and thus responsible for the safe-guarding of all Catholic teaching concerned with faith and morals, was the leader of the traditionalist group. He spoke in defence of Latin, showing as he did so his excellent command of the ancient language. He did, however, speak beyond the ten minutes allocated to each member who wished to address the council. The Dutch Cardinal Alfrink, who was presiding over the session on that occasion, warned Ottaviani that he was running out of time. When the Roman cardinal ignored him, Alfrink disconnected his microphone so that he could no longer be heard. There was a burst of applause from the assembly. Ottaviani, he who had been the mind of the Holy Office for nearly thirty years, was shocked and hurt and did not return to the council for some days. Pope John, who watched all the proceedings on close circuit television, often felt impatient with the long-winded speeches of the bishops. He did admonish the council this time, however, for the disrespect shown to the elderly cardinal.

The discussion on the subject continued for three weeks and it was agreed that bishops themselves should decide which parts of the Mass should be said in the language of their own countries. Now at last, authority was devolved upon the bishops. Previous to this, the curia had dictated the rules concerning the liturgy.

By the end of the first year of Vatican II it was clear that there was going to be a fair amount of turbulence in the church. Even the little world of the Scots College was given something of a shake-up. Monsignor Flanagan was gradually becoming disenchanted with what was happening at St Peter's. He had always been an enthusiastic liturgical scholar. Now he was hearing about the need for the renewal of the Mass rites and of Mass to be said in the vernacular. He was confused and neither he nor anyone else had any way of knowing what the ultimate style of the Mass was going to be.

Meanwhile, there was a problem in college of how to teach students to say Mass. It was obvious that alterations were going to be made and the students, especially those in the senior year, the prospective priests, were well aware of the winds of change. These young men were a formidable group, intelligent and eager and ready to break out of the strait-jacketed liturgy they had been taught, but it was some time before the Rector was able to conclude that their attitude was the right one. This period of confusion seemed to have more of an effect on the young men than on the older priests, and especially in those Roman colleges where the rubrics of the Mass had received extremely strict attention, with every last gesture having its own significance. Despite the clash of views between students and staff, there was no loss of discipline at the Scots College.

The proposed changes to the Mass were only the beginning. The bishops, many of whom were beginning to lose both the parochial attitude with which they had come and the awe in which they had previously held the curia, began to debate 'sources of inspiration'. Were the scriptures and the church's oral teaching both distinct ways in which God had revealed himself to mankind? For centuries the church had held that was so but Protestant churches regarded the scriptures alone as the source of revelation. Ottaviani led the commission investigation of this subject. He wanted to maintain tradition but his opponents felt that this would threaten the movement towards unity of the churches, a subject close to the Pope's heart. The more open-minded bishops also believed that the scriptures should be researched using modern literary and scientific methods in order to clarify them. Ottaviani's group opposed this, saying that the Bible should be read only with the guidance of a Catholic theologian. Eventually a new commission was formed to redraft a document on the subject which would both conform to Catholic teaching and be open to the views of other churches.

It was liberating for many of the bishops at the council to hear ideas and opinions which they had long held but were never empowered to articulate, being expressed and approved of in public. Out went the *Index,* the list of books which Catholics were forbidden to read. Out too went Pius IX's *Syllabus of Errors* which had condemned everything new. For too long the church had maintained an attitude of defence, safeguarding the sacred, regarding itself as separate from the world and the repository of the whole truth. It was now time to change the view that the church had nothing to learn from the world and put an end to excommunications, bans and anathemas.

Unlike his predecessors, Pope John was not concerned with condemning errors. During the council recess, he produced an encyclical entitled *Pacem in Terris* in which he proclaimed every man's right to worship God in accordance with the dictates of his own conscience.

He became universally popular with people of all faiths and of none. He read the signs of the times and saw that the church needed to examine its true purpose and its relationship with the world. The curia and the local churches had become distant from one another: he reintroduced the idea of collegiality. It would be up to his successor, Giovanni Montini, Pope Paul VI, to reorganise the curia and reconvene the council to look at the role of the priest, the religious and the lay person, for sadly, John XXIII died in the summer of 1963 when the work of the council had only just begun.

There was a feeling that nothing in the church would ever be the same again. The full impact of the discussions was not experienced until the documents were produced and translated and the bishops started to implement the ideas in their own countries. The business of renewal was an immense task and was to send shock waves through the Catholic Church during the sixties and seventies.

Tom Winning came back to Scotland at the start of this period of great change. Having spent five years at the Scots College, he began to think that he had been forgotten about by those back home. However, in 1964, James Scanlan, at the age of sixty-five, became Archbishop of Glasgow and Frank Thomson, whom Tom had met for the first time at the opening of the new college in the Via Cassia, became the new Bishop of Motherwell. In 1966 he recalled Tom to Lanarkshire, to take up the post of parish priest at St Luke's Church in Motherwell.

He was forty-one years old, still young, in those days, to be given what many priests longed for and would regard as having 'reached the top' if they were given it – their very own parish. The faith which Monsignor Flanagan and Bishop Scanlan had put in him had not been misplaced – he had been successful on the staff of the college and at the Rota. His health had continued to improve greatly since his surgery. It seemed that he must have been promotion material after all!

What lay ahead, at home in Scotland, was to be the biggest challenge he had faced so far – putting the theory of Vatican II into practice at grassroots level. It was certainly not going to be easy.

CHAPTER SIX

The Parish Priest

Brian Logue had been the curate at St Luke's for five years and Father Thomas Winning was to be his third parish priest in that time. This was rather a high turnover and, naturally, the young Father Logue wondered about his new superior. What would this new broom from Rome get up to? Would there be any 'aggro'?

He was right about there being a new broom, but there was no 'aggro' of any kind. The new parish priest did not give orders but worked out a way to share parochial responsibilities with his curate in what was a particularly deprived place, the Forgewood area of Motherwell.

The parish was small – only about eleven hundred people and from one end to the other about a fifteen-minute walk. Nevertheless there were many problems and much work for Father Winning and his assistant. Paradoxically, it was a community just getting together – the parish had opened seven years before Father Logue arrived – and a community which was breaking up. The root cause of this was the housing: blocks and blocks of maisonettes, soulless places without suitable amenities. There was a number of very low-income families, unemployed people and people who had no pride in their homes or their community. There was a great deal of vandalism and certain streets formed a disaster area where no-one was prepared to take the houses. As soon as the opportunity arose, people would get out of Forgewood because no-one wanted to bring up children in an area of family breakdown, of housebreaking and excessive drinking.

Many of the Catholics who were trapped in these poor conditions regarded the church as a total irrelevance and only sixty per cent of parishioners attended Sunday Mass. Tom Winning had to find a way to reach the missing forty per cent and make parish life more significant for them and for all the people in his charge.

He started with the children. St Luke's did not have a school of its own and shared the primary school with the cathedral. The cathedral children seemed to have a greater capacity for learning than those from poor homes or difficult family backgrounds, but Tom succeeded in persuading the less motivated children to become involved in the liturgy. Boys who seldom went to church at all were given a new impetus when he asked them to be altar servers, girls enjoyed taking part in Family Mass on Sundays when he asked them to read the scripture aloud or take part in the offertory procession.

He also tried to improve communication in the parish and prepared and issued a weekly bulletin containing instructions, announcements and some words of spiritual wisdom which he hoped would reach the hearts of his people. He made great efforts not just to administer the sacraments but to help people understand them and prepare for them in advance. Greater lay participation in the liturgy was strongly advocated by Vatican II but in Scotland change was implemented very slowly, if at all, and for some reason Bishop Thomson withheld permission for priests to change the position of the altar and say Mass facing the people. Once Tom had settled into his parish he went to see the bishop. He persuaded him that the change should be made in St Luke's, which was a very simple church, with little involved in moving the altar and realigning the sanctuary. Father Logue was pleased when his parish priest asked him to say the first Mass facing the people. This caused quite a sensation – it was a real novelty for everyone. Tom also experimented with the baptismal and funeral services and began to gain a reputation in Motherwell as a 'liberal' parish priest.

St Luke's was a poor parish, but its people were generous with their time and prepared to work for the church for its own sake and not for any personal glory. They had dances and socials and there was a nucleus of parishioners ready and willing to organise functions to bring people together and help them forget, for a little while, the drabness of their lives. St Luke's seemed like an oasis in an area of desolation: the little wooden church, the priests' house, the parish hall, formerly a stable, all set in large grounds with lawns and flowers.

Some of the local boys liked to use the church precincts as a playground and often incurred Tom's wrath as a result. Once, he gave some of them a particularly rigorous telling-off and on the Sunday morning following this occasion, the father of one of the boys approached Tom when he was on his way into the church and adopted a very threatening attitude. Another man was also on his way into Mass. He saw what was about to happen, (one 'Father' was going to set about another 'Father') came over, growled: 'You hit him – you hit me! Don't you dare hit the priest!' and shook his fist for good measure. The irate father beat a hasty retreat. The helpful parishioner turned out to be none other than Panty – the boy whose nose Tom had belted many years before in St Patrick's Primary, now a grown man with his own family. It would seem that when Tom hit Panty, he had made a friend for life!

The people of St Luke's grew to like their new parish priest. He was not known for his great oratory, breathing fire and demanding his congregation's attention, but he did project a quiet kind of power from the pulpit, reflecting the amount of effort he put into finding the right words to convey his message. Brian Logue learned a lot from him and was impressed by the way in which he tried to make the liturgy alive and meaningful, give people a different way to pray and avoid making religious practice a matter of routine. Despite all his efforts, however, after two years in the parish, Mass attendance had not significantly improved and Tom's concerns were compounded by the fact that Bishop Thompson decided to transfer Brian Logue to another parish in Shotts. 'When these men become bishops, they think they know everything!' Tom grumbled. Father Logue was disappointed too. When he went to Shotts he had to revert to saying Mass with his back to the people. The altar was marble so it was not as easy to change things as it had been in Motherwell. In fact no effort had been made in Shotts to implement any of the new ideas introduced by Vatican II.

This was the case throughout Scotland. Piecemeal changes were made in the liturgy but attitudes were not being changed at all. It was evident that the problem of renewal in the church was not going to be solved easily and this was the experience worldwide. Having Mass in the vernacular was one thing, but changing the whole 'model' of the church was quite another. The Catholic Church had been a monolithic, authoritarian institution for centuries, its members both priest-dependent and sacramentalist. Now people were told that, through their baptism, they too had a share in the priesthood of Christ. The clergy had to become used to a change of emphasis:

Vatican II was stressing their role in preaching the gospel and building up the community and the Christian faith – not just being available for church services. Both priests and parishioners had fixed ideas on the nature of the priesthood. The image of the church as a pyramid, with the laity as the base, priests and bishops forming the peak, and the pope at the top, was firmly ingrained in the Catholic psyche. It was difficult for many people to adapt. The change was confusing – even threatening.

Religious orders had also been called upon to revise and update the rules by which they lived. Communities of nuns discarded their medieval style habits for more modern dress, and some gave up the practice of wearing veils altogether. Many rigid regulations governing the daily lives of the religious were relaxed. The council had not produced any new definitions of faith but with the *aggiornamento,* the 'bringing up to date' which followed the sessions of Vatican II, it seemed that every other aspect of church life was being called into question. The ecclesiastical organisation which had always been a sure and stable point of reference for its people seemed to be turning into a 'runaway church'.

To add to the turmoil which Catholics were experiencing, all this was happening during the 'turbulent sixties', which, with the production of the contraceptive pill and, in 1967, the passing of the Abortion Act in Britain, became the age of sexual permissiveness. Pope John had established a commission to advise him and his council on birth control, and its members, except four, both clerical and lay, recommended to John's successor, Paul VI, that the church should relax its rules with regard to this. However, in 1968, Pope Paul VI published the encyclical *Humanae Vitae,* in which artificial forms of birth control were condemned and the church's traditional teaching upheld. His statement caused an uproar in the church; conservatives hailed the encyclical with approval but there were many others who regarded it as a retrograde step and who believed that Paul had undermined a great deal of what the council had done, dividing his own church.

Thousands of Catholics worldwide either left the church or simply ignored its teachings with regard to artificial forms of birth control. Priests, unable in conscience to forbid their parishioners to use the 'pill', left the church in great numbers. Many departed for other reasons: some could no longer see the need to be celibate, others , who saw no need for change in the church at all, experienced great crises in their own lives and, disillusioned, abandoned their vocations, with or without laicisation from the Vatican.

The traditional church in Scotland did not remain untouched by this period of confusion and uncertainty. A number of men gave up the priesthood, with Motherwell diocese suffering the greatest casualties. The influence which the clergy who remained had on their communities was waning. In the past, the church provided a social service for Catholics, the majority of whom were poor and suffered considerable discrimination. Now the people were more affluent, less subject to religious bigotry. The church societies and groups which had been formed to provide them with support no longer seemed necessary. Going to the bingo or the discotheque seemed far more appealing than going to religious services like Benediction or the St Anthony Novena. There was a small number of Catholics who pressed for a greater role in the church, questioning whether, among other things, celibate clergy had the competence to dictate to them on the subject of contraception and family life. But the Scottish hierarchy was in no hurry to implement change, feeling largely unprepared or indeed unable to guide its people through this crisis period.

If the bishops were struggling with Vatican II, then it was even more difficult for the ordinary priests to lead their parishioners through this transitional phase. For someone like Tom Winning, the situation provided a real career opportunity; he was indeed in the right place at the right time. Not for him any crises or dilemmas – he seemed to have no problem advising his parishioners to follow the papal line on contraception. He would never have considered disagreeing with the Pope, in public at any rate, on any moral or theological matters. This was a policy which, many would say later, was instrumental in helping him in his rise through the church ranks. So he was traditional when Rome was traditional, but when Rome said 'Update', he embraced the new proposals with enthusiasm. He had become very much a 'company man', agreeing with the Vatican that while the essential beliefs and traditions remained the same, the 'externals' of church life needed to be modernised if religion was not to go out of fashion altogether.

The church authorities must have thought that it was priests with just this attitude who were needed in the West of Scotland.

Tom had other 'advantages' too. Since his time in Rome as Spiritual Director, he had continued to attend the bishops' meetings as Minute Secretary. Thus he was privy to the hierarchy's discussions on the progress, or otherwise, of Vatican II developments in the country. The bishops were still very distant figures and few priests knew them personally. Tom Winning did and they trusted him. He still had his connections in Rome, of course, and while he was no genius, he did have the reputation of being a real grafter. All these factors were significant for a priest's *curriculum vitae,* and the gossip among the clergy was that he would not remain simply a parish priest for long. Soon he was appointed Vicar Episcopal, a new ecclesiastical post, with special responsibility for marriages in the diocese. He also became more immersed in the parish and at last his efforts seemed to produce some results.

Using some of the ideas of Richard Lombardi, a Jesuit whose 'Movement for a Better World' he had heard about when in Rome, Tom organised lay responsibility courses and different types of Sunday Evening Service, sometimes pulling in an attendance of two to three hundred. He built up a parish council and invited well-qual-ified speakers to talk to its members on aspects of Vatican II. But as before, he fell into the old habit of overworking and denying himself recreation. When he had first returned to Motherwell, Tom, John McQuade and two other priests would play golf in Lanark fairly regularly, but eventually his friends dropped him from their group because he always seemed to have some prior commitment on golf day. Tom's reaction was to blame the other priests for no longer in-cluding him. Such was his absorption in revitalising the church that he did not seem to realise that it was taking its toll personally – he was in danger of losing his friends.

This pattern of behaviour was to remain largely unchanged – no matter how long it took him to respond to correspondence, social invitations or telephone calls, he still expected friends to keep in touch with him and was genuinely aggrieved when they did not. This was perhaps, a result of his upbringing – although his family had not been affluent and he had not been spoiled in a materialistic sense, he was very much put on a pedestal by his relatives. Having a priest in the family was a great source of pride for Lanarkshire Catholics, particularly if he was good looking and personable, with the added glamour of having been trained in Rome. Tom Winning was probably quite used to his family thinking he could do no wrong and often failed to understand that not everyone would respond to him in that way.

His work rate may have harmed his social life, but it paid off in terms of his 'career' in the church. In 1969, the bishops asked him to prepare a memorandum regarding the establishment of a National Marriage Tribunal. Shortly after he submitted this, the tribunal was set up and he was made its first president.

This was both a prestigious and challenging appointment and he was pleased to be given the job. The tribunal was based in the south side of Glasgow, in Woodrow Road, Pollokshields. Now Archbishop Scanlan would be his boss again.

Tom had not spent any time in Glasgow since his short spell in the seminary at Bearsden and was largely unfamiliar with it. He wondered what the big city had in store for him.

Little did he know.

CHAPTER SEVEN

The Auxiliary Bishop

'The Archbishop of Glasgow's here and will be circling George Square until you find a parking place for his Mercedes.'

Whenever the Commissionaire at the City Chambers heard these words, he did not need to be told twice. If James Donald Scanlan had arrived for a grand civic occasion, then that meant business. The words and the chauffeur who said them were now familiar, as was the VIP who would shortly be making an entrance. The Commissionaire looked lively, a place for the sleek black car was found right away and then Scanlan swept into the Chambers, dressed in full episcopal regalia. His violet silk mantle sweeping out behind him, he would look every inch the archbishop, the representative of the city's Catholic community.

In the six years since 'JD' had been at the helm of the archdiocese, this scene had been enacted many times. Just as in Motherwell, one of his chief interests lay in improving the relationship between the church and the civic authorities and he had been successful in this, by means of his own unique style.

Archbishop Scanlan dressed to impress. His opulent items of apparel were intriguing to those who were unfamiliar with them. He used them to draw attention to the dignity of his role and, in a theatrical way, bring the archdiocese recognition. Eventually, Vatican authorities deemed the more formal prelate's wear to be out of date and the archbishop, the Sandhurst man, found he had to put away what, for him, had become the equivalent of a full dress uniform. By that time, however, the City Fathers had discovered that the flamboyant churchman, a presence whom they had become accustomed to seeing at their official functions, was an intelligent and urbane person and they respected him. The university awarded him with the degree of Doctor of Divinity but it was not only politicians and academics upon whom he made an impact. Despite his love of standing on ceremony, he sometimes proved that he had the 'common touch' when it came to understanding his fellow Glaswegian.

The best example of this was in January 1971, when a tragic event occurred at the Rangers versus Celtic match at Ibrox Football Stadium in the Govan area. Sixty people, all Rangers supporters, were killed in a terrible crush on the terracing. Since their foundation, rivalry had existed between the two clubs with much attendant and acrimonious bigotry. Archbishop Scanlan's response to the disaster was to arrange Requiem Mass at St Andrew's Cathedral in Clyde Street to pray for the dead and their families. In itself, this was not extraordinary but the fact that he asked both Celtic and Rangers Football Clubs to attend was certainly significant. Rangers, who, it has to be said, were not known for the number of Catholic players on their books, to attend Mass at the Cathedral? Unheard of! What was the archbishop thinking about?

Yet Scanlan's gesture proved to be masterly. Davie White, the Rangers manager, accepted his invitation: the whole club would attend the Mass. This was nothing short of sensational. Were the secretarian barriers which had existed for so long going to be broken down? Certainly an atmosphere of goodwill was created in Glasgow. The dignity of the human person was being given precedence over the colour of his football scarf.

After this, everyone knew the name of Archbishop Scanlan and for some in the west of Scotland, his well-judged act seemed to be more momentous than the recent promotion of Scanlan's fellow archbishop in St Andrews and Edinburgh, Gordon Gray, to the rank of Cardinal. Paradoxically, it seemed as if Scanlan, despite his remote, medieval prince-bishop style, had his finger on the pulse of Scottish religious life.

Within the archdiocese, however, the archbishop had his critics who thought his form of leadership was as much a relic of the past as his style of dress. He had been appointed at the age of sixty-five and was considered by some to be too old for the job. In terms of Vatican II renewal, the pace of change in Glasgow was slow, the status of women in society was not being reflected in the church, and lay people in general still played only a peripheral role in archdiocesan life. Whilst Archbishop Scanlan agreed with the principles of Vatican II, he felt it would be up to a younger man to put them into practice.

Moreover they did not really fit in with his concept of the function of a bishop. As far as he was concerned, the bishop was in charge and everyone else, priests and lay people, had to obey him.

Scanlan had by no means been idle during his episcopate. Since he had succeeded Donald Campbell, seventeen new parishes had been established and seven new churches built in existing parishes. A religious education centre had been opened and a chaplaincy established at the new Strathclyde University. Nine more religious orders became based in the city. The archbishop tried to keep up to date with population movement in the archdiocese and, although the volume of building work had tapered off since the fifties, the church had established a substantial physical presence. Scanlan had inherited considerable debt from his predecessor, who had made the decision to have a new seminary built in Cardross. This cost the church an enormous amount of money – all its investments had to be realised to pay for it. But for some of the more so-called 'intellectuals' within the laity, church expansion, the archbishop's efforts to create a positive image of the archdiocese for outsiders, and his ecumenical gestures were not enough. They challenged Scanlan, wanting the church to renew itself from within. Some of the more radical formed 'The Scottish Catholic Renewal Movement' in an attempt to change things themselves.

So when Tom Winning came to Glasgow to work at the National Marriage Tribunal, the city was fast becoming a centre of theological debate. The 'Renewal Movement' invited many well known speakers to the archdiocese.

Catholic professionals, nuns, clergy and students both clerical and lay, turned out to hear theologians like Hans Küng, Edward Schillebeeckx, Karl Rahner, Enda McDonagh and Daniel Berrigan. Local Protestant theologians like Professor William Barclay took part in debates as did members of parliament such as Norman St John Stevas and David Steel. At no time did the Movement have the approbation of Archbishop Scanlan, indeed its members were asked to remove the word 'Catholic' from its title as Scanlan deemed the views expressed by some of the visiting speakers to be unorthodox and unrepresentative of the church's stance. Ordinary Catholics did not like it either; they felt it was only for the middle class 'intellectuals' and had no bearing on the lives of the majority of parishioners. They also found the confrontation of lay people with the archbishop both upsetting and confusing, as they had for so long been used to taking what members of the Renewal Movement described as a 'subservient' role. The Lay Apostolate Council, set up by the hierarchy to 'advise people on their mission in the church' did not solve any problems either, as its members were specially chosen by the clergy and, rather like the Renewal Movement, it was, to all intents and purposes, a 'closed shop'.

Somehow, the whole church in Glasgow would have to be renewed, according to the principles of Vatican II and be led by someone who had the knowledge and vision necessary to devise a strategy for what was obviously going to be an immense task. James Donald Scanlan knew he was not that person, so in 1971, when he was seventy-two years of age, he announced that he was looking for a co-adjutor bishop who would succeed him when he retired.

The priests of the archdiocese duly received letters, from the archbishop's office, asking their opinions as to who they thought would be a suitable candidate for the role of co-adjutor bishop. Tom Winning never received a letter, nor was he ever asked his opinion on the matter. Although he was based in Glasgow he was still a priest of the diocese of Motherwell and every weekend he would return to Lanarkshire to say Masses in any parishes which needed help. During the week, at the office in Woodrow Road, Pollokshields, he worked with five other priests, on marriage cases, with a secretary to help them. He himself lived above the office, employing a housekeeper to assist with the domestic duties. He had little time to be involved in general archdiocesan affairs though did join in the gossip with the other clergy in the tribunal office at lunchtimes.

'I've had a letter about the co-adjutor bishop,' said one of the priests, Father Chalmers, looking up from his soup one day. 'I think the curia have all had theirs now and the Canons. Mine was delivered by the archbishop's chauffeur.' 'Well', Tom said, in reply to this, 'The man who gets that job will have his life shortened by a decade at least!'

The months passed and Tom thought little about the matter until 19 October. He had been at a Ministers' Fraternal – a meeting of priests and clergy of other denominations – with Father Pat Brady, parish priest of St Albert's, Pollokshields, and returned to Woodrow Road where Mary, the secretary, advised him that he was to phone the Apostolic Delegate, Archbishop Enrici, in London. 'Blast!' he thought, 'I haven't paid those taxes for the marriage cases.' Hastily preparing an apology, he got on the phone. The Delegate had never spoken to him before. It must be serious!

In London, Monsignor Carson, the Delegate's Secretary, took the call. 'Oh yes, Tom. Hold the line. The Delegate would like to talk to you.' 'Hello, are you alone?' 'Yes, your Excellency.' 'The Holy Father would like you to accept the post of Auxiliary Bishop to the Archbishop of Glasgow.' 'I thought it was a Co-adjutor...?' 'No, the Holy See has decided it's to be an Auxiliary Bishop and the Holy Father would like to invite you to accept this post. Do you accept it?' 'Well, I've never really thought about it, your Excellency. I wonder if I could have some time to think about it and I'll phone you back.' 'No, I must have an answer now!' 'Well, if it's for the good of the church, Yes!' 'We could make the announcement in one week's time, the 25th. O.K. You'll get a letter and I'll inform the archbishop...'

Tom was in shock.

Lunch that day was chops, turnip and potatoes. All he could do was push it around the plate. He could not eat a thing! There was no one he could talk to about the appointment before its announcement except Archbishop Scanlan and he was not available. His thoughts turned to his sister and her family. When the news came out they would expect him to have a little celebration in Woodrow Road. The housekeeper, Mrs McInnes, would have to have some advance notice of that. He told her he wanted to have a Hallowe'en party for twelve to sixteen people on 25 October. She looked sceptical. He felt guilty. What else could he do? He had to tell a 'little white lie'.

He also had another worry. His former mentor and parish priest, Monsignor Hamilton, was dangerously ill. Tom felt that Alec Hamilton was one person who should know of his appointment as soon as possible, despite the rules. Suddenly, Monsignor Hamilton died and Tom had hesitated a day too long. The funeral was on 25 October, the day that the appointment could be made public. Present at the Requiem were Archbishop Scanlan, Bishop Thomson, Tom himself and many other priests and parishioners of St Mary's, Hamilton, including Tom's sister Margaret.

Archbishop Scanlan instructed Bishop Thomson to announce

the news about his new auxiliary at the end of the Mass. Neither Tom nor Bishop Thomson liked the idea but Scanlan was insistent. At twelve o'clock, just as the bearers were turning the coffin to carry it down the centre aisle, Bishop Thomson publicly announced Father Tom Winning's appointment as auxiliary bishop. Tom had been in St Mary's parish for years. Everyone knew him. The announcement caused a buzz of interest in the congregation and, he felt, took attention away from his old friend. So far as he was concerned, the timing was unfortunate. It was not his wish to take anything away from Monsignor Hamilton in death.

Tom's sister Margaret was giddy with shock when she heard the news. Her brother – a bishop! Father John McQuade escorted her to the Chapelhouse for a cup of tea and a chance to absorb the idea. Back in Pollokshields, the staff at the tribunal were opening little notes which Tom had left with his housekeeper to hand to them personally. By late afternoon, the whole archdiocese had heard and lay people and younger priests speculated as to what the new bishop would be like. Another man from Motherwell? In the same mould as Scanlan perhaps?

The senior clergy who had nominated him knew better of course. His work in Motherwell, having earned him the reputation of being 'progressive', showed that he had an understanding of the changes necessary to implement the conciliar documents. He had considerable pastoral experience and was also a canon lawyer. A Glasgow man he was not, it was true, but he was known to have a personable manner and a sense of humour which Glaswegians would appreciate. Those who knew him found him direct and forthright and even brusque, on occasion. At forty-six, now the youngest member of the Scottish hierarchy, he would present a new image of the bishop: he seemed the ideal person to update the Archdiocese of Glasgow.

The day after the big announcement, Archbishop Scanlan offered Tom a choice of rings from the strong room of the archdiocese. Most of the episcopal jewellery in Glasgow belonged to Charles Eyre, a wealthy Englishman who had been archbishop from 1878 to 1902. Tom selected one of his heavy, old gold rings set with an amethyst. He received the other symbols of his new position, the mitre and crozier together with the full title of 'Auxiliary Bishop of Glasgow and Titular Bishop of Louth' at a ceremony held on St Andrew's Day

1971 in the cathedral in Clyde Street. It was an awesome occasion for him, the attainment of the fullness of the priesthood. He believed he could rise to the challenge which the mitre, crozier and ring symbolised: that he would be both teacher and pastor of the Archdiocese of Glasgow to which he was now wedded. He felt a new surge of spiritual enthusiasm: now he would have an opportunity to implement the ideas of Vatican II and bring the hierarchy and the people closer together. However, it was not going to be as simple as that.

The first problem which he encountered lay in the nature of the position of auxiliary bishop. From a spiritual point of view, he is as much a bishop as the man in charge but he lacks authority to make decisions. An auxiliary only has as much clout as his archbishop chooses to confer upon him. It did not take Tom long to realise that, although he could see what needed to be done, he would not be allowed to make any changes in policy. He began to realise that Scanlan was disappointed because the Holy See had not given him a co-adjutor with right of succession and equal authority to himself, but merely another auxiliary like Bishop James Ward. Ward had originally been an assistant bishop to Archbishop Campbell. When Scanlan returned to Glasgow, Ward found himself in a difficult position – he had no legal status in the archdiocese. The new archbishop remedied this by making Bishop Ward vicar general and parish priest of Holy Cross Church. The Holy See chose not to give Ward a diocese of his own. He remained 'titular' bishop of a defunct See.

He took over the day to day administration of the archdiocese, a subject in which Scanlan was not interested, and soon he held the purse-strings. This gave him kudos and he guarded the position jealously. Only Monsignor Francis Coyle was privy to archdiocesan business. As far as Bishop Ward was concerned the new Bishop Winning was going to have nothing to do with it. He had not forgotten what had happened in Rome during the council, when he was excluded from the hierarchy's meetings, while Winning was brought into them as Minute Secretary.

Tom had a second problem. Archbishop Scanlan was two years away from retiral and Bishop Ward was sixty-eight. Tom seemed almost a boy by comparison and given any encouragement might well rock the boat. Scanlan and Ward agreed with the ideas of Vatican II in principle but were in no hurry to effect the great changes necessary to bring the archdiocese into line with them. Thus they treated the new bishop correctly but coolly, almost as if they wanted to dampen the fires of his enthusiasm.

Tom was concerned lest he should be appointed to a parish like Bishop Ward and he told Scanlan that he did not want to be tied down in this way, he wanted the whole archdiocese to be his 'bailiwick'. However, Scanlan had other ideas. The week after Tom's ordination, the parish priest of Our Holy Redeemer's, Clydebank, died suddenly and the archbishop told Tom that both he and Ward thought he should take over the parish. Tom could only agree but with the proviso that he replace the two curates with men of his own choice. He had nothing against the curates themselves but requested this as a point of principle, feeling sure that if he did not take some kind of stand, he would be overruled on subsequent issues. Scanlan agreed to the change in personnel and after three months, Tom left the Marriage Tribunal in Woodrow Road and moved to Clydebank. It was his senior curate, Father John Muldoon, who was delegated to handle the bulk of parish administration, for Tom was determined to be bishop first and foremost and get to know all the people of Glasgow as soon as possible.

He went to the curial offices in Park Circus two days a week but from the outset was to find himself completely excluded. Bishop Ward made little or no effort to involve him in diocesan discussions, appointments, finance or even handling the mail. In addition, changes were made and decisions taken affecting Dumbartonshire without his being informed, despite the fact that Archbishop Scanlan had indicated he wanted Tom to be given special care of that area. Eventually, Tom decided to go into the office early in the morning and open the mail himself. Then he retired to his room to write sermons or attend to his own correspondence. The frustration became almost unbearable. He asked Bishop Ward if he could go through the mail and discuss diocesan business with him but Ward would have none of it. Tom wondered how he could communicate policy adequately if he had never been involved in its making. He would be seen by the archdiocese as an executor of policy yet he himself knew nothing about it.

His exasperation grew as the months passed. When he had first been appointed Scanlan had taken him around the main areas of the city introducing him as the 'Staff of his ageing being' but the archbishop soon lost enthusiasm for that and left Tom to 'gang his ain gait'. This is exactly what he decided to do. Paradoxically, his exclusion from archdiocesan administration led to him becoming the most well-known and accessible of the Glasgow bishops. He embarked on a series of weekend visits to all the parishes in the city, met with the priests, stayed with them, said Mass on Sunday, visited the local schools and the sick and returned to Clydebank on Monday. This was his programme for two years. Neither of his fellow bishops appeared to show any interest in his activities which were well-documented in the Catholic press. On one occasion Scanlan did suggest that perhaps he was doing too much, but that was all.

Tom also tried to channel his energies into effecting change where he could, particularly in the area of religious education. In the years which had elapsed since the closing of Vatican II, Catholic teachers had become increasingly confused by the changes and, bereft of the Catechism and the staple *Hart's Christian Doctrine,* no longer knew for sure what they should be teaching the young Catholics in their charge.

Prior to Vatican II, religious education was supervised by some twenty to thirty priests who 'inspected' schools in the archdiocese at regular intervals to evaluate their 'RE' provision and content. Some of the priests worked at this for five days a week over six months of the year but it was a very benign kind of inspection, designed to upset neither the teachers nor the children. As new ideas were disseminated from Vatican II, the 'inspectors' quickly lost credibility.

As auxiliary bishop, Tom Winning joined the Council of Priests in Glasgow and immediately persuaded them to set up a small committee – of which he became a member – to visit four or five 'pilot' schools to interview Head Teachers and staff. Each of their reports had one significant point to make: secondary schools required full-time chaplains. Tom was not surprised by their findings. Two years before he was was appointed bishop, he had been present at a meeting when four secondary Heads had made a similar request to Archbishop Scanlan. Scanlan had turned them down, saying that as there was a shortage of priests it was impossible to provide chaplains for schools. Bishop Ward, a traditionalist, who had also been present at the meeting, was aghast when one of the Head Teachers suggested that perhaps they could have an occasional Mass in the school. The bishop stated that the place for Mass was the church and that it was not possible for it to be said anywhere else. Tom knew that reintroducing the subject of school chaplains was not going to be easy but decided on the bold approach. He would not ask the archbishop to appoint chaplains, he would tell him. He rehearsed his speech and approached Scanlan with a firm manner which belied his inner trepidation: 'Your Grace, we need chaplains for the schools. I've prepared this letter for the appointment of twenty-four of them. Will you please sign it?'

Surprisingly, Archbishop Scanlan signed the letter without demur, perhaps sensing the determination of his auxiliary. Soon twenty-four schools, some as big as parishes in population, had chaplains appointed on a fulltime basis. This was a source of great satisfaction for Tom although he was aware that school chaplains were not uncommon in other dioceses; where Glasgow was unique was in the large number of priests appointed. Clerics from other countries, visiting Glasgow, approved the enterprise but could not see the manpower involved being committed in their own dioceses. In reaching his decision, however, Tom reasoned that he was simply redeploying the priests. He felt that, because of the large number of young people attending the schools – over one thousand and two thousand in some cases – it would not be possible for a priest to maintain worthwhile contact with pupils if the chaplaincy was only to form part of his normal duties.

So it was that Tom Winning began to find a role within the archdiocese by confronting particularly difficult problems and dealing with them. He felt that he had to do something with the Lay Apostolate Council, for example, which had lost its way in the post Vatican II confusion. Convinced that it needed as much 'shaking-up' as the schools, he met with its members and as a result, some of its executive retired, others took their place and the whole group made a serious study of the Vatican documents related to the role of lay people in the modern world. A plan for the future development of the council was drawn up which encouraged its members to look outwards to the people in the parishes rather than inwards to themselves as an exclusive group. His aim was to make a 'breakaway' renewal movement for lay people unnecessary. Change should and could come from within, under the auspices of the church.

The university chaplaincy had also become something of a thorny problem in the archdiocese and had been going its own way without reference to the archbishop and the local church. This reached a crisis point when the chaplain, Gerard Hughes, a Jesuit priest, incurred the disapproval of Archbishop Scanlan because he gave communion to non-Catholics at interdenominational services. Hughes was threatened by dismissal but Tom Winning intervened and suggested to the archbishop that a Chaplaincy Commission be set up which would give the chaplaincy freedom of operation but also ensure that the archdiocese had some role to play in commenting and perhaps advising on what was done there. It proved to be a creative solution. Hughes was kept on as chaplain, the archbishop was respected because he had been seen to change his mind, his desire for 'formality' in chaplaincy life was appeased because his auxiliary would chair the commission and the student body was satisfied because its chaplaincy was regarded as equivalent to a parish and the students now had more say than before in the organisation of church affairs within the university community.

Gradually, the frustration which Tom had initially experienced in his new role started to diminish. To a large extent he was still being 'frozen out' in the archdiocesan office but that did not seem to matter quite so much, now that he was succeeding in making changes more or less independently. He was getting to know people and losing his complex about being an 'incomer'. Bursting with pent-up energy, he became involved in everything he could, in order to find an outlet for it. Before long, he found himself immersed in one of the more unusual processes of life in the Catholic Church, which if it had not been for the effects of the Reformation in Scotland, should actually have taken place in 1629, some three hundred and fifty years earlier.

CHAPTER EIGHT

The Miracle in Easterhouse

'I hope to come to Glasgow again and do some good in it.' So said John Ogilvie, a Jesuit priest, in 1615, shortly before he was found guilty of treason and hanged at Glasgow Cross. Had he 'returned' to Glasgow, in 1967, and done something very good indeed? It fell to Auxiliary Bishop Winning to find out if he had. In 1972, Tom was asked to lead an investigation into a claim that an unemployed docker, John Fagan, a Catholic living in the deprived area of Easterhouse, had been cured of terminal stomach cancer through the intercession of the long dead Jesuit. A miracle? In the twentieth century? And in Glasgow? Surely not. The Catholic Church is notorious for its reluctance to describe any event as miraculous without first scrutinising the evidence meticulously. An important part of the examination is the Apostolic Process, which, in accordance with long-standing custom, is held in the diocese where 'divine intervention' is said to have occurred. The investigation into the events in Easterhouse was the first apostolic process to be held in the Archdiocese of Glasgow.

A tribunal was set up, in the offices adjoining Archbishop Scanlan's residence in Park Circus, to question witnesses associated with the alleged miraculous cure. Scanlan, as archbishop, should have been the judge at the tribunal, but in view of his health, which was starting to decline, and the tiring nature of the task, he appointed his new auxiliary *Judex Delegatus* – Judge Delegate – to question the witnesses on his behalf. The result of the tribunal's investigations would help determine whether John Ogilvie, already regarded as 'Blessed', would be the first Scot to be canonised a saint since Queen Margaret in 1250.

Canonisation is the church's official declaration that a deceased person had led such an outstandingly holy life that he or she is suitable for Catholics to imitate and ask to intercede for them with God.

People who have died in defence of the Catholic faith – martyrs – and those who have furthered learning and understanding – doctors of the church – have been made saints. Trying to decide who is truly a saint is a long and difficult process. The Vatican has a department devoted to the procedure, called The Congregation for the Causes of Saints. If a miracle, for example a cure for which absolutely no medical explanation is possible, can be proved to have taken place as a result of prayers made to a holy person whose 'cause' is being investigated by the church authorities, then this can often be regarded as the clinching evidence that the person is worthy to be called 'saint'. For someone who is considered to have died a martyr's death, one cast-iron miracle would help to put him or her on the road to canonisation. The Jesuit John Ogilvie came into this category. For a variety of reasons, his 'cause' had been on the Vatican's books for a very long time.

Ogilvie was born near Keith in Banffshire in 1579. His grandfather had been treasurer to the Catholic Mary, Queen of Scots, but John, like his parents, was a Calvinist. With the Reformation, Scotland was becoming a Protestant country and it was increasingly difficult and dangerous to hold the Catholic faith. However, while he was on the continent to further his education, John gave up Calvinism and became Catholic, as his ancestors had been. He went further than this and was ordained a Jesuit priest. He was determined to return to Scotland and help out the Catholics who were having a hard time of it. Ogilvie's superiors were not keen on the idea as the Monarch, King James vi of Scotland and i of England, had decreed that it was a treasonable offence to be found saying or hearing Mass. Priests were kicked out of the country and those found to be giving them safe houses faced persecution. It was a risky business but Ogilvie did go back to Scotland, for the first time in over twenty years, arriving on the east coast, wearing a disguise, in 1613.

Ogilvie did all he could to help the beleaguered Catholics, particularly in Edinburgh and Glasgow. He tried to remain *incognito* when he was not with his 'flock' but there were spies and informers everywhere. In Glasgow, a man pretending that he wanted to return to Catholicism betrayed Ogilvie for a large reward, to John Spottiswoode, who had been appointed Episcopalian Archbishop by King James.

If it had been just the matter of being a priest and saying Mass, then Ogilvie would simply have been banished, but there was more to it than that. Like the rest of the Jesuit order, Ogilvie disagreed with the King's belief that he and not the Pope should have authority over the church. The Episcopalian Church was used by James like a Department of State, helping him rule. John Ogilvie was loyal to the King but asserted the authority of the Pope over baptised Christians.

As a result of this assertion, Ogilvie was held in prisons in both Glasgow and Edinburgh. He was denied sleep, prodded with sharp instruments, punched, had his hair pulled out and was thrown about his cell. In spite of months of torture, he did not betray the Catholics with whom he had been in contact nor did he agree that King James had the power to deny them their right to freedom of worship. On trial for his life, he still would not repudiate the Pope. So James VI and I sentenced him to death and he was hanged at Glasgow Cross, in March, 1615, having been found guilty of treason.

To Catholics, Ogilvie was a martyr; news of what happened to him was carried throughout Britain, Scots forced into exile made sure that his story was told on the continent, and by 1629, the Jesuit order was making representations to the Pope for John Ogilvie to be canonised a saint. But there was no Catholic hierarchy in Scotland, no seventeenth-century equivalent of James Scanlan or Tom Winning allowed to conduct the apostolic process and investigate Ogilvie's life, which would have been the next stage of the proceedings. The cause of the martyred Jesuit would have to wait until the anti-Catholic laws had been repealed, the Scottish hierarchy restored and the twentieth century well established.

Monsignor William Clapperton (who would later be Tom Winning's Rector at the Scots College in Rome) became the chief mover and shaker – officially the Postulator – behind the John Ogilvie affair during the 1920's. Throughout that decade, Glaswegian Catholics, on the anniversary of Ogilvie's death, had walked, in prayer, from the Tolbooth at Glasgow Cross to Glasgow Cathedral, praying that there would be progress in his cause for canonisation. Their prayers were heard when, in 1929, Pope Pius XI declared that John Ogilvie was to be called 'Blessed' and that people could pray to him for 'favours'. However, it would take, literally, a miracle for Ogilvie to be made a saint. Some forty years later, John Fagan from Easterhouse, the chief witness to come before Bishop Tom Winning during the apostolic process, claimed that he had been the recipient of just such a miracle.

Fagan was ill at ease when he came to the Park Circus offices in November 1972. He was unnerved by the courtroom atmosphere and the formal nature of the proceedings, established right at the start when he was required to swear an oath: '...to declare truthfully what I have, to preserve secrecy about the questions asked and my replies, so help me God and these Holy Gospels'.

He could hardly be blamed for feeling nervous. Here he was, an ordinary man from a working class background, facing a bishop, a doctor and a priest who wrote down everything he said. What he was saying was that God had intervened in his life and he had been cured of an incurable disease. His replies to the 'Interrogatories' – questions specially prepared for Tom Winning by the Vatican Congregation for the Cause of Saints – were barely audible at times. His wife Mary, the second witness, was as nervous as John but their story was absolutely compelling.

John Fagan first realised that he was seriously ill in 1965, when he was diagnosed with stomach cancer. He had an operation and appeared to make a recovery, but by November 1967, he became seriously ill again and the doctors and surgeons at the Royal Infirmary in Glasgow could do no more for him. One of them advised his wife to 'take him home and be good to him'. Another suggested that she should get John admitted to the Hospice in Clydebank. The family doctor, John MacDonald, had agreed with this, telling Mary Fagan that looking after a dying man was going to become very difficult. She had been adamant that whatever needed to be done, she would do herself.

John wasted away from nine stone to five, a far cry from the man who had worked at the dock-side. By the end of January 1967, he was unable to eat anything and could not raise his head without assistance. On the evening of Saturday, 4 March, Doctor MacDonald visited his patient for what he assumed was the last time. Fagan had been vomiting in the most terrible way and the doctor tried to prepare Mary for what was the impending death of her husband. He told her that he would be back on the Monday morning to sign the death certificate. There was nothing else he could do for John now.

The night passed and Sunday came. People visited the house all day long and said prayers for the moribund Mr Fagan. They prayed to John Ogilvie. The Fagans were members of Blessed John Ogilvie

Parish in Easterhouse. Their parish priest, Father Thomas Reilly, had for years been following every reference to favours attributed to the parish patron and had enlisted the help of his curate, Father John Fitzgibbon. Fitzgibbon had asked the parishioners to pray to Ogilvie for John Fagan. By his own admission Fagan was a lukewarm Catholic but that made no difference to the priests and parishioners in Easterhouse. A medal depicting Ogilvie had been pinned to Fagan's pyjamas.

Throughout Sunday night, Mrs Fagan sat alone by her husband's bedside. About six o'clock on the Monday morning she suddenly realised that there was no sign of breathing from John or evidence of any pulse. 'That's it,' she thought, 'he's gone.' She continued to sit, slumped in the chair. Some time elapsed and then with no warning at all, she heard her husband's voice saying: 'Mary, I'm hungry.'

Mary was shocked to the core. She could not believe it. She hurried to the kitchen, boiled John an egg and with shaking hand, fed some of it to him, a little at a time. 'I feel so different,' Fagan said. 'I thought you were dead, John,' said his wife, 'I really thought you were dead.'

Doctor MacDonald came to the house some time later, as he had promised he would. He was astounded. 'That man should be dead!' he kept saying. Father Fitzgibbon was the next visitor. The man whom he also had expected to find dead was sitting up, drinking tea. Aghast, Fitzgibbon turned to Mary Fagan and said: 'I believe the hand of God is in this house!'

Seven years later, called as the third witness in the apostolic process, Father Fitzgibbon stated that this was still his conviction. Doctor MacDonald, who had attended to John Fagan at every stage of his illness, was also a witness. He was not a Catholic but as far as he was concerned, there was no natural explanation for the recovery of his patient, John Fagan.

A number of other medical witnesses were called, as and when they were available, during the six months duration of the process. It had been Father Reilly who had enlisted their help, when the word 'miracle' had first spread throughout his congregation. He felt the best way to deal with parish gossip and satisfy the people and himself was to have the case properly investigated, with John Fagan and Doctor MacDonald's agreement. Father Reilly had an official role to play in the cause of John Ogilvie. He assisted Father Paul Molinari, a Jesuit from Turin, who had taken over the role of Postulator.

Molinari's advice from Rome was for Father Reilly to appoint a medical panel. He warned that any evidence for a miracle would have to be irrefutable or it would be dismissed at once by the Vatican. Three doctors from Glasgow agreed to form the panel, a senior General Practitioner, a consultant and a senior lecturer from Glasgow University. Their job was to find a natural medical explanation for Fagan's recovery. They were Catholics but each one of them was sceptical about the case and believed it would be possible to explain the 'cure'. Religious beliefs did not influence their judgment and details of the meticulous way they had gone about examining hospital records, biopsy and x-ray reports and interviewed medical and surgical staff, came out during the interviews at Park Circus. But they could not explain why John Fagan had got better. Further investigation had also been carried out by other eminent medics, specialists in the field. This had been at the insistence of Livio Capocaccia, Professor of Gastro-Enterology at Rome University and Secretary of the Vatican Medical Tribunal, during meetings with Fathers Molinari and Reilly. Two consultants in the same field as Capocaccia, one from the Southern General Hospital in Glasgow and the other from Edinburgh University had been brought in.

A number of theories had been examined in an endeavour to explain the recovery. The first of these, spontaneous regression of the cancer, that is natural forces in the body destroying the malignant cells, was investigated for months but was eventually rejected as the recognisable features of such natural regression could not be found in this case. Another theory was that there had not been any cancer in the first place but another not necessarily fatal growth. This, together with a number of other theories, was investigated and dismissed. John Fagan was given a series of tests by the consultant in Edinburgh and his report to Father Reilly's medical panel, which in turn reported to the tribunal, was that the patient had had recurrent gastric carcinoma, was now free of all signs and symptoms of the malignant disease and no satisfactory explanation could be given. Professor Capocaccia's doubts were dispelled when he came to Scotland himself to review the whole case with the Edinburgh specialist and by 13 April 1973, Bishop Winning was able to draw the apostolic process to a close. The evidence, including the medical reports, had been translated into Italian and, with Archbishop Scanlan's seal affixed to it, the whole dossier was delivered to Father Paul Molinari in Rome.

The matter did not end there. Molinari then had to make a precis of all the material which would be examined by two independent medical experts in Rome. If they were to reject the case, notwithstanding the work of the Scottish doctors, then the Medical Commission, a body of perhaps nine to fifteen doctors, appointed by the Vatican, would not have the evidence brought before it. However, if there was to be a favourable response then the case still had to be presented to the theologians, with one, known as the Devil's Advocate, concentrating on all the objections possible to John Fagan's recovery being a miracle.

If the theologians concluded that divine intervention had brought about the cure, it still remained for the Pope to ratify the case. Then and only then would Ogilvie be declared a saint.

Whatever the final outcome, the experience of John Fagan, the faith of the people of Easterhouse, the collaboration of churchmen and medical men and the apostolic process which brought all these things together, constituted a remarkable episode in the history of the archdiocese.

All that interested parties in Scotland could do now was wait and see. Surely the file on John Ogilvie would be closed soon? Yet if there had been a miracle and he was canonised it would not be an ending but a beginning – worldwide interest and a real publicity coup for the church. It might mean a fresh start for those who had lost interest in religion and maybe bring in some new recruits...

Endings and beginnings were to be a keynote during 1973 and 1974.

On 21 October 1973, Tom Winning received a phone call telling him that Bishop James Ward had suffered a heart attack. Dutiful to the last, Ward had refused to go to his bed until he was sure that Tom could perform his confirmation duties for him. Half an hour after the first call, Tom received another, informing him that the bishop had died.

It was the beginning of the end of the pre-Vatican ii era in the archdiocese. Within a few months, Archbishop Scanlan, seventy-five years old, announced that he was retiring.

The Archbishop asked his auxiliary's opinion about his successor. For Tom Winning there could only be one man for the job, his friend in Rome, Monsignor Rogers. Scanlan was pleased with Tom's reply.

'That would be my choice too.' he said. 'You're too young. Maybe next time!'

Unbeknown to Tom, it was not his youth which Scanlan had highlighted as the reason why he should not be promoted to archbishop. In a report to the new Apostolic Delegate, Bruno Heim, he described his auxiliary as being 'weak in authority'.

Archbishop Heim asked the Glasgow priests to nominate three people whom they considered to be suitable candidates to replace James Donald Scanlan. Tom Winning sent a memo to the delegate, giving an account of the present condition of the archdiocese, based on his experience as auxiliary. He told Heim that the person Glasgow needed was Monsignor Rogers. He spent a fortnight working on the memo and sent it off to the Delegate's office in London. Within a couple of days he received a phone call from Heim. The document was very interesting, he told Tom. Could he come to London as soon as possible?

It was a bright day in April 1974, when Tom Winning arrived at the Delegate's office in Wimbledon. He met the Secretary first, who said: 'Come into my office when His Grace is finished with you and we'll have a chat.' 'I could be a while – I've got a lot of stuff here, things to add to the first memo.' The Secretary laughed. 'He won't be interested in that,' he said, 'Go on in. You won't be very long.'

Tom entered Bruno Heim's office and when he sat down the Delegate drew up a chair beside him and said: 'The Holy Father wants to know if you will accept to be Archbishop of Glasgow?' This did not sink in. Tom started to open his briefcase. 'Your Excellency, I've come down to talk.' The Delegate interrupted. 'It's all settled, you only have to say 'yes'.'

This was an even worse shock than the phone call from the previous Delegate three years before. When at last he could speak, Tom was characteristically laconic. 'Well,' he said. 'All right!'

Bruno Heim then mixed a very strong cocktail, a skill for which he was well known, and handed it over to the bemused archbishop-elect. After a brief conversation and some little time to recover, Tom found himself on the homeward flight to Glasgow. He picked up transport on his arrival and was soon on his way to Croy for a confirmation visit. No one else knew that he had been in London for the day or that his time as auxiliary bishop was over.

CHAPTER NINE

The Archbishop of Glasgow

The announcement of Tom's appointment was scheduled for 13 May 1974, when the Apostolic Delegate was to concelebrate Mass in St Andrew's Cathedral. For the next three weeks Tom had a hard time keeping a secret which, apparently, not even Archbishop Scanlan knew about. He lay awake night after night, trying to visualise the future and what everyone's reactions might be. Even if he had a lot of co-operation, he would now be very much on his own. However, he consoled himself with the fact that he, more than anyone, perhaps, knew what Glasgow needed. His priority would still be going out and about as much as possible and continuing to be accessible to people.

Bruno Heim and his secretary arrived in Glasgow on 11 May. Archbishop Scanlan, together with his secretary and Tom Winning, formed the welcoming party at the airport.

'Now I'll tell the archbishop about you!' the Delegate said in a quiet aside to Tom before he joined Scanlan who was waiting in the Mercedes. Tom helped the secretaries load the luggage into his own car which was to be taken by them to Scanlan's house in Park Circus.

When he jumped into the archbishop's plush limousine and sat in one of the tip-down seats opposite the two Prelates, Heim said to him: 'I've just been telling His Grace that you are his successor.' Archbishop Scanlan looked directly at Tom, then turned to the Delegate and said: 'Well, as I was saying...' and continued the story he had been relating to him before Tom had entered the car. He did not offer congratulations nor shake hands, nor make mention of the matter later in the evening.

Tom Winning was familiar with Archbishop Scanlan's idiosyncratic manner, nevertheless he felt a wave of disappointment sweep over him. His mind started to race. Was Scanlan unhappy that he had succeeded him? Perhaps he didn't really want to think that he was having to give up the job and someone else was taking over. Perhaps he was thinking

'Big deal!' After all, he was now seventy-six and had been appointed to the position of archbishop at an age when most men were retiring. But surely it would have cost him nothing simply to say: 'Well done'?

The next evening, after dinner which had followed Mass, the Delegate made sure that only bishops were present when he announced the new appointment to members of the hierarchy. The first to congratulate Tom was Bishop Thomson, followed by the others, with one notable exception.

On Monday, 13 May, at a meeting of clergy in Notre Dame College, Dowanhill, the Delegate publicly announced the name of the new Archbishop of Glasgow. There was an immediate and spontaneous standing ovation. The Delegate explained that the choice had not been a random one. Recommendations had been sought from bishops, priests, leaders of religious orders, Catholics in public life and various other clergy and lay people in Scotland.

'I emphasise to you that he is your choice,' said the Delegate, 'These recommendations were all characterised by a deep personal concern for the pastoral good of the archdiocese and by the spirit of charity in which they were put forward.'

The new archbishop responded to the Delegate's speech with a brief address. He was still hurt that 'JD' had not acknowledged his new position in a personal way but he did not show it, making allowances for Scanlan's age, pride and old-fashioned outlook.

'Our thoughts are with His Grace, Archbishop Scanlan today,' he said. 'He has been my mentor over a number of years and his combination of dignity and charm will long be remembered. I hope he will be our companion for many years to come. He will always have a hundred thousand welcomes in this archdiocese.'

To enthusiastic applause, he continued:

'It's a real pleasure to me to realise that I will be serving the warm-hearted people of Glasgow ... I am proud to be their archbishop. I also thank the Holy Father for his confidence and trust in me.'

At the age of forty-nine, most priests would be hoping to be given their own parish. Only five months earlier, Tom had celebrated his Silver Jubilee as a priest and now he was being given charge of one hundred and five parishes and forty-two religious communities. He was to be the sixth Archbishop of the See of St Mungo since the restoration of the hierarchy in 1878.

A few days after the official announcement, he asked Archbishop Scanlan where he would like to stay. 'Here, in Park Circus,' Scanlan said, 'but this place is too big for me – there are three levels.'

The old man was suggesting that the two archbishops should live in the same house but Tom Winning did not like this idea, saying he preferred accommodation with a garden. He may also have had the notion, of course, that his predecessor's proposed arrangement might cramp his own style considerably. Despite Tom's complimentary words about Archbishop Scanlan, there had been no reciprocal congratulations – indeed there never were to be any expressed in the future – so it seemed only sensible for each of them to live separate lives.

Although Tom could rationalise Scanlan's attitude it continued to jar him emotionally. But another, much darker cloud shadowed his life at this time too.

Monsignor Gerard Rogers had been one of the first to hear about the new archiepiscopal appointment and had been delighted by the news. Tom, however, was shocked when, on the phone to his old friend in Rome, he heard him stuttering and stammering. Gerry had consulted Italian doctors to investigate this sudden and alarming inability to speak properly but nothing was found to be wrong. It was on a visit to the Middlesex Hospital in London that he was told he had a tumour on his brain. The swash-buckling Monsignor, whom both Tom Winning and James Scanlan had seen as the ideal candidate for the role of Archbishop of Glasgow, had only months to live. It was to be his friend and protege who would officially assume the role for which Gerry himself seemed tailor-made, at a ceremony in St Andrew's Cathedral on 6 September.

The installation was a festive occasion. A pipe band in Clyde Street played 'Scotland the Brave' while police marshalled the crowds who had gathered to cheer outside the cathedral. Scouts and Guides formed a guard of honour as Cardinal Gray and the rest of the hierarchy, priests of the archdiocese, the Lord Provost Sir William Gray, magistrates and councillors processed into St Andrew's. There were provosts from Dumbarton and Lanarkshire, the Chief Constable, Sir David McNee, the Lord Justice Clerk, Lord John Wheatley and several MPs. Priests and nuns attended, and every Catholic organisation had one or more representative. A fanfare of trumpets rang out from the choir loft as the new archbishop entered the cathedral. Monsignor

Coyle, who was the Archdiocesan Chancellor, read aloud the papal document of appointment and, via radio, the voice of Stephen McGill, Bishop of Paisley, was heard in thousands of homes as he installed the new archbishop, presenting him with the book of gospels and the pastoral staff:

> In the name of God, I, Stephen, Bishop of Paisley, do install you Thomas, Archbishop of the church of Glasgow. May Our Lord Jesus Christ watch over you henceforth and for ever.

In his first homily, the new Archbishop expressed the great sense of responsibility he felt and also what he saw as the task of the archdiocese. There was a sense of urgency in his words:

> … Pope Paul has entrusted me with the church of Glasgow. One day, God will ask me what I made of it. If this church is to take up the challenge of the present hour and be Christ's church in the last quarter of the twentieth century, we have to be more than ever in Glasgow a knowing, loving and serving community …

He called for:

> … an openness to the Spirit of God, a rejection of bigotry and discrimination based on religion … unity of doctrine will be of little avail if we have not learned to live together and love one another in our daily lives – no matter what our faith may be …
> Every generation has its own contribution to make to the confirmation of Christ's work, a contribution which can be made by no other. What has to be done now has to be accomplished by us or it will never be done at all …

Tom Winning's direct words and manner went down well with newspaper reporters who wrote about his appointment.

'He looks and sounds like the kind of chap you'd be glad to meet having a half-pint at the local,' wrote Neville Garden in *The Daily Express,* 'And if that sounds disrespectful … it isn't meant to be. Nor I imagine, will Archbishop Thomas Winning see it that way … for he is not a man who stands on ceremony or wraps himself in a flurry of golden words. He is a cheerfully disposed man of the people …'

'He is concerned that people will be able to look on him as an ordinary man,' reported James McKillop in *The Glasgow Herald,* 'He recalls that, up until his appointment as bishop, he was always nervous of meeting bishops. Even today, he does not call bishops older than himself by their Christian names …'

Tom's pawky sense of humour also increased his personal appeal. He took as his archiepiscopal motto the words: *Caritas Christi urget nos,* 'Christ's love urges us on', but observed archly that *Christus vincit,* 'Christ is winning' might have been more appropriate. The image of the archdiocese was immediately revitalised by his appointment and many Glasgow Catholics celebrated the fact. Nevertheless, the champagne corks had barely stopped popping when it became clear that, while the new archbishop wanted to be approachable and on good terms with his priests, he also meant business. He called a meeting of the clergy and spoke on some twelve different topics ranging from the relationship he hoped to have with them to the standard of dress he deemed appropriate for them.

He stressed his expectations of one hundred percent co-operation from his priests and expressed disapproval of the Catholic clergyman's habit of making critical opinions about the archdiocese which went no further than the 'smoke-filled rooms of friends'. He advocated that these comments be expressed openly, provided they were constructive. 'Opinions bandied about which are cynical, derisive and divisive are not worthy of men in our position,' he told them.

He gave instructions concerning the modernisation of the liturgy and the importance of the proper presentation of Mass. 'We do not subscribe to the cult of the scruffy,' he said 'and we must not be merely half prepared.'

He outlined plans for Glasgow priests to go the the Scots College in Rome for a month's Refresher Course to update themselves on Vatican II and he also had some advice concerning their daily lifestyles. 'You cannot do a good day's work if you are out regularly to all hours of the morning. Nor does this give good example. No decent citizen is constantly outside his own home after midnight. I leave the rest to your own conscience. Every man is entitled to his day off in the week, but let's hope he works hard on the other days.'

The Lay Apostolate, the University Chaplaincy, the position of seminaries and archdiocesan finances were also dealt with by the archbishop and he made his views on Catholic education quite clear: 'There is pressure from outside to integrate Catholic schools. As far as I am concerned it is not integration but disintegration if that happens because we would be integrating with nothing!'

He ended his talk on a rallying note, telling the priests that the rest of the Catholic community in Scotland looked to Glasgow for a lead and that it should and could provide it. 'At College I took part in the play *Macbeth*', he said to them, 'I now recall as very appropriate, when Macbeth had suggested the possibility of failure to his wife, Lady Macbeth replied: 'We fail? But screw your courage to the sticking place and we will *not* fail!' That's the slogan I pass on to you now. Let us work together then, in a spirit of friendliness and freedom!'

It was not long before the new archbishop was implementing radical changes in diocesan administration. He had felt that one of the great weaknesses in the system was that the clergy was, more or less, devoid of any kind of responsibility apart from work in the parish. Priests were never given the opportunity or encouragement to have any kind of diocesan involvement. The clergy lacked initiative, enterprise of any kind had always been frowned upon. Now he devised a way to let the priests see that Glasgow was their diocese, not just his, to enable them to share responsibility in order that the church might be run more effectively. The key to his plan lay in the office of 'vicar episcopal'.

Fourteen priests were appointed to take charge of areas for priority treatment in the life of the local church. These comprised: Communications, Ecumenism, Fabric and Planning, Justice and Peace, Vocations, Youth Council, Lay Apostolate, Liturgy, The Marriage Advisory Council, Missionary Awareness, Religious Education, Schools and Education, Religious Orders and Congregations. These new 'vicars episcopal' would hold the posts for two years and Tom suggested that it could be decided whether they would be subject to election by the Priests' Council. The new VEs were to be regarded as the archbishop's delegates, acting with his authority and assisted by committees of laity and priests, so that many more people would be involved in these areas of responsibility. The plan had its roots in the documents of Vatican II, particularly those related to the nature and life of the church.

A third vicar general was appointed, Tom's boyhood friend, Charles 'Donny' Renfrew, now titled 'Monsignor' who joined Michael Ward and John Gillespie, the senior priests of the archdiocese. Tom's decision to have Donny work closely with him was widely approved, as the former seminary Rector was known to have a range of skills complementary to those of the archbishop; he was independent, quite unafraid to speak his mind to Tom Winning and had the respect of both priests and people.

One of the first of the fourteen priority areas to be given a high profile by the new archbishop was ecumenism. Pope John XXIII had led the way by inviting Protestant leaders to the first sessions of the Vatican Council, but efforts to promote dialogue between the churches in Scotland had been somewhat fragmented. In 1975, Tom was instrumental in bringing the faltering ecumenical movement a great step forward when he accepted an invitation from the Church of Scotland to address its Assembly, the official gathering of its ministers. Since 1969, a Catholic observer had been invited to attend this annual meeting of the national church. Not all Protestants approved of this new practice, particularly the members of an extreme group led by Pastor Jack Glass, and invariably they would appear outside the Assembly building or in the gallery with banners, the slogans on which would express their outrage at the presence of 'Popery' in the Church of Scotland's precincts. They were appalled when they heard that Tom Winning had been invited, not only to be present but also to speak to the Assembly on 21 May 1975, the first Roman Catholic archbishop to do so. A minority in the Assembly itself opposed the invitation but it could be counted on to receive the Catholic guest with courtesy. It was Pastor Glass who made the Moderator (the President of the Assembly) and the officials very nervous in the period prior to the archbishop's visit. What would happen? Would a potentially major religious event end up as nothing but an unholy row?

Archbishop Tom Winning found the whole prospect daunting too, as he wondered how best he could express himself to the Church of Scotland, how his words would be received or if indeed the hecklers would allow him to be heard at all. Before writing this address, he discussed some of his ideas with Father James Quinn, a Jesuit from Edinburgh, who had been involved in ecumenism in Scotland for a number of years, and with Ronnie Walls, who had been a Church of Scotland minister before becoming a Catholic. Tom was determined that the words he expressed at his installation as archbishop, calling for 'a rejection of bigotry and discrimination based on religion' should be translated into action and those like-minded in the Presbyterian Church were giving him an opportunity to do so. Suspicion and antipathy based on religious differences had scarred

Scottish history: bigotry would not be destroyed overnight or indeed over decades, but at least the channels of communication could be opened and barriers gradually brought down. The two churches had not spoken to one another 'officially' for over four hundred years. It was time for the silence to be broken, no matter what the dissenters felt about it.

The event, broadcast on national television, proved to be a resounding success. Pastor Glass and his followers were handled skilfully by the Very Reverend Andrew Herron, an official at the Assembly, who refused them entry and refunded the Pastor the ticket money for gallery seats. Tom received so much applause on his way up to the dais that, in one of his characteristic moments of self-questioning, he wondered whether what he had to say would come up to the expectations of those present. He had opted to wear a black frock-coat, similar to those worn by ministers at the Assembly, instead of the customary purple of the archbishop. He also chose not to wear his pectoral cross in order to avoid alienating anyone present by a display of ceremonial dress, emphasising a difference in style between the two churches. Within the first minute of his speech he realised there were not going to be any interruptions and that he had the full attention of the Assembly as, on behalf of the Catholic community, he thanked the Church of Scotland for its cordial invitation.

'What do brothers say to one another after years, and in our case centuries, of estranged silence?' he asked them. 'Surely they ask forgiveness?' Then he drew upon the words used by Pope Paul VI to the observers from the different churches at the Vatican Council: 'If we are in anyway to blame for the long years of separation we humbly beg God's forgiveness. And we ask pardon too, of our brethren, who feel themselves to have been injured by us.'

For our part we willingly forgive the injuries which the Catholic Church has suffered and forget the grief endured during the long series of dissensions and separation.

... I believe it is through misunderstanding of what is expected of us that some hesitate to commit themselves wholeheartedly to work for Christian unity, seeing in it, perhaps, a threat to an already deeply-held personal faith.

God never asks the impossible. What he does ask of us is obedience to what we sincerely believe to be the revealed word of God,

a serious respect for the beliefs of other Christians and sincere acknowledgement that they are our brothers in Christ. It's a rough
road and there are stumbling blocks for all. We, for example, in
the Roman Catholic Church, realise that we are a stumbling
block to other Churches because of our convictions regarding the
nature of the church and her authority.

Nonetheless, we are fully committed to working with you and the
other Christian churches towards unity for we are confident that
the Holy Spirit will guide all of us to an ultimate solution …

The address concluded to the sound of thunderous applause.

'You have won our hearts!' said the Moderator, the Reverend
James Matheson, from Skye, as he shook the archbishop's hand, and
he went on to quote the words of John Wesley: 'I don't say come to
my side nor draw me to thine. But if my heart is now thy heart in the
love of Christ, then give me thy hand!'

It was an emotional moment and a turning point in interchurch
relations. Ironically, Tom's superiors in the Vatican seemed to be
rather piqued that he had managed to bridge four centuries of history
by means of some straight forward words and without consulting
them. A copy of Tom's address was sent to Rome via the Apostolic
Delegate but it was lukewarmly received. One of the questions asked
in the Secretariat of State headed by Cardinal Benelli was: 'Did he
have a theologian helping him to make this up?'

It took a letter from Archbishop Willebrands of the Secretariat for
Christian Unity, reporting on Tom's background, education, qualifications and presumably his 'Romanità', to settle any queries raised by
Benelli's department. Nevertheless, the event at the Assembly received
little publicity in Rome and the address was not printed in the English
language version of the Vatican newspaper, *L'Osservatore Romano*.
Perhaps the Scottish archbishop had stolen the curial thunder?

Whatever the reason for the lack of enthusiasm in Rome, in
Scotland the address was well received and Tom invited the
Moderator, James Matheson, with whom he developed an immediate rapport, to speak to the Catholic Lay and Priests' Councils in
Glasgow. He now felt more confident to press on in building up
good relationships with the other churches in Scotland. However, he
was correct in predicting that there would be stumbling blocks on
the road. Having a 'serious respect' for the beliefs of others was

difficult for some people. For example, the following year, when Pope Paul VI decided that John Ogilvie was indeed to be canonised a saint, Robert Kernohan, the editor of the Church of Scotland magazine, *Life and Work,* wrote questioning the doctrine of sainthood and that of mediation (the belief that saints can intercede with God on one's behalf) held by the Roman Catholic Church. James Matheson said that Mr Kernohan was expressing personal views and not those of the national church, but support for Kernohan came from Professor William Barclay, the well-known biblical scholar and Presbyterian author, as well as Professor James Whyte, Convener of the Church of Scotland Inter-relations Committee.

The canonisation should be abandoned, it was suggested, the raking-up of the past could only do harm to the ecumenical movement. John Ogilvie lived at a time when the Protestant persecution of Catholics was severe. Those days were past; in the interests of unity, surely his activities and his death should not be glorified in this manner?

The issues gave rise to some correspondence in the press but Tom Winning did not become embroiled in any controversy. He continued to feel that ecumenism must never attempt to water down sincerely-held religious beliefs and made a brief public statement to the effect that 'patient and enlightened discussion had been the hall mark of joint conversations between the Catholic Church and the Church of Scotland in recent times' and 'he trusted that these would continue.' Tom's understanding of Ogilvie was that he had died for ideals acknowledged by both Catholics and Protestants alike: freedom to worship without penalty and persecution, and spiritual freedom of the church from state control. The fact that he died for his principles should not be concealed in shame but highlighted with pride.

Pastor Jack Glass felt strongly enough about the canonisation to make his way to Rome for the event. He and his companions were present in St Peter's Square on 17 October, 1976 to voice their protest. They were outnumbered, however, by the thousands of pilgrims who had come to celebrate the occasion and to hear Paul VI send his greetings to all Scots, Catholics or otherwise, telling them that he shared 'the joy and pride of all Scotland at the supreme honour paid to a beloved son of your land'.

John Fagan, the man through whom the event was made possible, was a special guest, along with his wife, the doctors and the priests of

the parish involved in his case. Fagan's 'miracle cure' was the newspaper story of the year in Scotland and representatives of the press
were present at the Vatican to report on what was for the Scottish
Catholic Church, the culmination of a process lasting three hundred
and fifty years. Sir Angus Ogilvy and his wife, Princess Alexandra, together with other members of the Ogilvy/Ogilvie families were there
to remember their distant kinsman, and Peter McCann, then Lord
Provost of Glasgow, started the celebrations the day before the
canonisation by hosting a reception for the Scottish bishops and lay
guests in the Grand Hotel on Via Vittorio Emmanuelle Orlando.
Jesuits, both from Scotland and elsewhere, also took the opportunity
to mark the occasion and said a Mass of celebration in the Gesù, the
Mother Church of the Society of Jesus in Rome. Representatives
from the Episcopalian Church in Scotland were also present at the
ceremonies together with members of the Russian Orthodox Church,
in true ecumenical style.

Absent from the proceedings was the man who probably would
have revelled in them most: Archbishop Scanlan. He had died, suddenly and unexpectedly, in March 1976, three weeks after returning
to London to take up a chaplaincy in the Tyburn Convent in
Marylebone. He would have been proud to see Glasgow in the limelight during the Ogilvie celebrations. JD had been a larger-than-life
figure in the church in Scotland. Tom Winning regretted his passing,
despite the old man's reaction to his appointment. He could not say
Scanlan had been his friend – he had been his mentor, to some extent, but for the most part, he had been his archbishop in the unique
way in which Scanlan himself understood and lived out that role.
Without doubt, the church would never see his like again.

It was during this same year, 1976, that Tom Winning saw for the
first time, another man who was soon to have an influence on his life.
He had been invited to Philadelphia, to a Eucharistic Congress, a
series of religious ceremonies, lectures and conferences. On the
opening day of the Congress, sitting in the sanctuary of the city's
cathedral, he was struck by the appearance of a cardinal directly opposite him. This man seemed to tower above all the rest, with his
firm, resolute face and hair of a pale blonde colour which curled up at
the sides. He had high cheek bones and the kind of strong counten-
ance which, to Tom, was reminiscent of a painting of some medieval

pope. When leaving the cathedral Tom asked someone: 'Who is that man?' The answer was: 'That's the Pole, Wojtyla.'

The impression the cardinal made on Tom was further reinforced when, at one of the big Masses during the Congress, he preached for an hour in a most erudite manner. Tom thought that Wojytia was obviously an outstanding individual, recalling that he had been one of the leading thinkers and speakers at the Second Vatican Council. He hoped he would have an opportunity to meet him one day.

Improving archdiocesan communications became a priority for 1976 and Tom established a monthly publication, a newspaper entitled *Flourish,* in order to do this. His original idea was that the fourteen vicars episcopal should contribute a half-page report for every issue to keep the diocese abreast of what was going on in each area of responsibility. As well as that, he intended to contribute every month himself and genuinely felt that this would solve the problem of communication and co-ordination of activities in the archdiocese. He was very soon to be proved wrong, for a number of reasons.

Not all of the fourteen men were communications orientated and producing written reports was difficult for them. For others, the nature of their area of responsibility, for example, education, made it impossible to report in the public domain all the details of meetings and discussions held in private. Verbal reports to the archbishop himself were much more appropriate for them. However, although Tom was eager and willing to talk to each of these fourteen men at any time, he was to find that, as he himself became increasingly involved in other church business at the level of the Bishops' Conference, it was not always easy for him to be accessible to them. The appointment of the vicars episcopal had generated fervour and activity, but somehow the system was not coming together in the way Tom had at first envisaged. The original idea of *Flourish* communicating the work of all fourteen agencies in the archdiocese and all his activities as well did not succeed. He now knew that the church required something more effective to bring together these disparate groups and aspects of archdiocesan life, and once again in his career his thoughts turned to pastoral planning as the ultimate answer to his co-ordination problems. Obviously, appointing fourteen vicars episcopal and putting them in charge of different areas was not fundamental enough: the archdiocese required a plan for action and renewal which would take it into

The young Tom Winning, aged ten.

The Winning family: Tom with his parents and sister Margaret.

Scots College students with their distinctive soutanes and 'soup plate' hats. Tom Winning: first left.

Father Tom Winning:
Ordination Day,
18 December 1948.

After an audience with Pope Pius XII in 1949.
Tom Winning third from the left.

Monsignor Gerry Rogers, friend and mentor to the young Father Winning in the nineteen fifties.

Archbishop James D. Scanlan, Archbishop Thomas Winning, Cardinal Gordon Gray on the occasion of Thomas Winning's installation as Archbishop of Glasgow, 6 September 1974.

Archbishop Winning addresses the General Assembly of the
Church of Scotland, May 1975.
Photograph from the Scottish Catholic Observer.

Pope Paul VI meets John Fagan and his wife at the canonisation of
St John Ogilvie in October 1976.

Pope John Paul II at Murrayfield Stadium, Edinburgh, May 1982.
Photograph from the Scottish Catholic Observer.

Cardinal Thomas Winning having received his 'red hat' from
Pope John Paul II, November 1994. *Photograph from Flourish.*

Cardinal Winning celebrates with his people in Rome.
Archbishop Keith O'Brien is on his right.
Photograph from Flourish.

Cardinal Cahal Daly of Armagh (left) and Cardinal Basil Hume of Westminster (right) with Cardinal Tom Winning as he celebrates fifty years in the priesthood, January 1999.

the eighties and nineties. However, having served only two years as archbishop, he felt that the time was not yet right for such wholesale re-evaluation of church life in Glasgow and kept the idea 'on hold', to be drawn upon later.

He did not abandon *Flourish,* which continued to be published monthly, serving as a 'serious-popular' means of communicating events of significance in the archdiocese and a vehicle for dialogue and discussion. Some parish priests thought that being asked to sell *Flourish* was an imposition and those in poor parishes told the archbishop they thought it should be a free publication. Other parish priests were very successful in selling copies.

It was neither easy nor cheap to produce such a paper, nor was it possible for its format and content to suit everyone. Some of its issues were and continued to be very effective in drawing the public's attention to the plight of the needy, perhaps none more so that the one published in March 1977. 'If this picture shocks you, we're sorry, but …' was the front page headline of that edition and the picture referred to was that of a small boy, David Lopez, sitting beside Tom Winning. Instead of a nose, the boy had a gaping hole in the middle of his face. The accompanying report explained that Archbishop Winning was making an appeal to the people of the archdiocese to help pay for the plastic surgery necessary to restore the child's features.

David's parents were Campa Indians who lived in the remote area of the Andean jungle in Peru. At the age of three months, David, a sturdy baby, was bitten on the face by a sandfly. The resultant infection caused severe damage to tissue and bone, leaving the child seriously disfigured. When tribal medicine failed to halt the disease, David's father took him on a hazardous canoe trip from the village of Shima to Puerto Ocopa, where there was a mission run by the Franciscan order. He was looked after by the nuns until they could get him on a small plane to the children's hospital in Lima. The boy was accompanied by his father and the mission's padre.

Tom Winning came to be involved with David Lopez when he received a letter from Dr Ian Jackson, a plastic surgeon in Canniesburn Hospital in Glasgow. Dr Jackson, who had never met Tom Winning before, told him that he had just returned from Peru where a Swiss nurse had drawn his attention to a small boy with a hole in his face and pleaded with him to help the child. Dr Jackson had been interested in the case, but knew that a long series of operations would be required to help the boy. These could be carried out in Canniesburn, his home base, but a lot of finance would be involved.

This was the big snag: money. It was not possible to carry out the operations under the National Health Service without setting a precedent which could open the floodgates to requests for treatment from many parts of the world. Dr Jackson had made contact with the Save the Children Fund and similar groups but without success. Now he was turning to Archbishop Winning of Glasgow for help. The immediate need was for £2,000 to get things started. Tom wrote back to Dr Jackson telling him that he himself did not have £2,000 but there would be no problem in raising the money. He told the doctors to bring the child over and make a start on the surgery and the church would meet the expense of it. Subsequently, he heard from Jackson that, with hardly any warning, Martine, the Swiss nurse, had brought the child to Scotland. Tom asked Father Thomas Gibbons, who was in charge of childcare in the diocese, to liaise with Dr Jackson. While on his rounds of pre-confirmation visits to schools in the city, Tom Winning told the children of the little boy whom he had met and how he was going to have a lot of operations on his face. It was a very moving story. He did not ask the children for money for David, but when their Confirmation Days came round they brought gifts and cheques to Tom for the Peruvian boy and sent a tremendous number of 'Get Well' cards to him in Canniesburn Hospital.

Dr Jackson, a member of the Church of Scotland, had written to Tom because David had come from Peru, a Catholic country. He was delighted when the archbishop made an appeal through the columns of *Flourish,* and the *Glasgow Evening Times* acted similarly. Both Jackson and his wife strongly opposed the idea of publishing photographs of David showing his deformity, they did not want him to be regarded as some kind of freak. An exception was made for Tom Winning who believed there are times when it is necessary to give people a jolt, an opportunity to understand the suffering of others. The photograph of David and the Archbishop of Glasgow, taken in Canniesburn Hospital, and its publication in *Flourish* had the immediate effect of encouraging an overwhelming response to the plea for help. £46,000 was collected for 'The Boy David'. The Jacksons decided to adopt David and took him to America where Dr Jackson went to take up a new hospital job. They kept in touch with Tom Winning for some time. He admired them both greatly, but he was disappointed that David was not brought up as a Catholic.

The columns of *Flourish* were used by Tom Winning to take preliminary steps towards the appointment of two auxiliary bishops. He had been working on his own for three years, administering the diocese, making day-to-day decisions, attending functions. There were approximately sixty confirmation ceremonies scheduled for 1977, a work load too onerous for one man. Through *Flourish,* Tom invited priests and people to write to the Apostolic Delegate, Bruno Heim, indicating their choice for bishop – three names in order of preference, stating brief reasons for selection. Several hundred people replied.

Tom Winning himself had two priests in mind for the posts when he first approached the Delegate about this matter. Nevertheless, he was determined to go ahead with the process of consulting the people of the diocese. His article in *Flourish* read:

Since my appointment to this See, I have always envisaged working with assistants. You might call this Phase Two of our plan for the archdiocese. Phase One was carried out with the appointment of Vicars Episcopal and the restructuring of the deaneries. To lead an archdiocese like Glasgow can never be a one-man job.

When the Apostolic Delegate had collected the replies, he prepared a list showing, in order of preference, the names of those selected. When he advised Tom how the 'League Table' stood, the latter was pleased to note that his own selection, Donny Renfrew and Father Joseph Devine, the vicar episcopal for the laity, were at the head of the list. After finding out more about the nominees from the priests and people most closely acquainted with them, it was up to Heim to make his own choice of three names for submission to Rome. The final result was as Tom Winning expected. At the beginning of May 1977, Donny Renfrew and Joe Devine were appointed auxiliary bishops to the Archbishop of Glasgow. Tom still had not got through all the confirmations and, before he was due to address parents in Drumchapel, had lost his voice completely. Bishop-designate Renfrew was thrown in at the deep end and spoke on the archbishop's behalf. Donny and Joe were ordained later that month in St Francis's Church, Cumberland Street, in the Gorbals, where sixteen hundred people packed the pews to witness a 'double ceremony' the like of which had not taken place in Scotland for ninety-nine years. (In May 1878, Charles Eyre, then Archbishop of Glasgow, consecrated the Bishops of Argyll and the Isles and Galloway just two months after Pope Leo XIII had restored the Scottish hierarchy.)

'We have a great future in the church in Glasgow,' Tom said at the ceremony. 'Under the leadership of your three bishops, may clergy, religious and laity pray together and work together in their pilgrimage towards the new and eternal city of God.'

He encouraged his two auxiliaries to go through the same process he had worked out for himself, visit the parishes for weekends and get to know the people. He wanted them to take a wide view of their work, not confining themselves to the kind of 'territorial patch' which had been his experience as an auxiliary bishop. They should be present in the whole diocese as he was, and neither he nor they should feel excluded from any part of it.

With two assistants to help him, the Glasgow clergy thought that their archbishop might slow up his pace of activity a little, for he had earned himself the reputation of being something of a human dynamo. He was always 'on the go', never turning down an invitation to celebrate Mass, attend a meeting, give a talk. He seemed indefatigable. As a younger man his appetite for work often made him physically sick but now he seemed to thrive on it. He liked being in charge and, although he had Donny Renfrew and Joe Devine to ease the load, he did not relax at all. Quite the contrary: freed as he now was from the burden of administering all the confirmations in the archdiocese alone, he channelled his energies into other areas, fast becoming an outspoken champion of the poor and needy in the city.

He decided to shelve a plan to renovate and extend St Andrew's Cathedral, choosing instead to spend ninety per cent less than the estimated cost simply on essential repairs. He felt the money should be used for more important matters. In *Flourish* of June 1977, he wrote:

For some time I have been concerned at the increasing hardships being experienced due to unemployment and economic cuts. Glasgow is already the most deprived city in Britain; it follows, therefore, that we are the most deprived diocese. While proud of the work carried out by so many organisations within the church on behalf of the elderly, the sick and the handicapped, the young and destitute, I look at the deprivation around us and ask, what is the church doing about it?

The answer is: not nearly enough.

There is no doubt we need a new and modern cathedral ... plans have been put to me for a two-stage renovation and extension of St Andrew's costing almost £2 million altogether. But I can't go ahead with a full-scale renovation when so many of our fellow citizens are suffering so much. The church is concerned with the whole person and not merely the building of churches ... I have decided we can do without a new cathedral meantime and I believe we should concentrate our energies instead on other aspects of the church's involvement with people.

It was in 1977 that the Archbishop Winning Charity Ball was held for the first time, raising £10,000 for sufferers of Spina Bifida. The intention was that the Ball should be held every year in one of the Glasgow hotels and that the proceeds should go to a different charity on each occasion: the homeless, the elderly, the mentally handicapped and other needy groups. This was an original venture in the church in Scotland, though in Chicago, Cardinal Cody had been the patron of a similar enterprise. It proved very successful and the 'Archbishop's Ball' was to become a popular date in the archdiocesan social calendar – with middle-class Catholics at least. Tom Winning had no trouble in persuading them to part with thousands of pounds over the years in order to help the underprivileged of Glasgow.

The archdiocese's annual pilgrimage to Lourdes gave him an opportunity to spend time with the sick and the mentally and physically disabled members of the church community, and in a pastoral letter he focused attention on their needs. A new technique related to the spiritual formation of mentally handicapped children and adults, known as SPRED, was developed in the archdiocese, respite homes provided and social and spiritual activities co-ordinated throughout the city. The pastoral and social welfare branches of the church in Glasgow were beginning to burgeon in different directions and Tom became President of the Commission for Social Welfare. He never hesitated to speak out about injustices in other countries too, commenting publicly in 1978, on the violation of human rights in Argentina. Similarly, until an eleventh hour withdrawal of charges, he was ready to fly out to support Archbishop Denis Hurley of South

Africa, who had been summoned to stand trial for making what were described as 'false accusations' about South African police's treatment of civilians in Namibia.

CHAPTER TEN

Home and Abroad

As well as establishing himself and his ideas in Glasgow, Archbishop Tom Winning also found that he had to play a role on the wider church stage. Bishops are required by statute to pay a visit to Rome every five years to report on the progress of their diocese: the so-called *ad limina* visit, meaning 'to the threshold'. Some will also represent their countries' hierarchies at the large assemblies of bishops from all over the world known as 'Synods', to discuss certain aspects of church life. Tom attended his first Synod in Rome in 1977, the subject of which was the religious education of young people. He was given the opportunity to address the international gathering and express his views on catechetics, in Latin, as the rules demanded. The month-long Synod was exacting but provided the kind of intellectual stimulus which he loved. He got to know many other bishops, particularly those in the English-speaking group and often found himself in lively discussion with the Archbishop of Liverpool, Derek Worlock, who was to become a good friend. Tom stayed at the Casa del Clero, a large hotel for clergy, rather than in the Scots College. This was solely for convenience as the college was situated far out from the city centre while the Casa was only twenty minutes' walk from St Peter's.

The visit to Rome was not entirely devoted to work; there were some opportunities for socialising and it was on one of these occasions that Tom met the cardinal whom he had seen at the Eucharistic Congress in Philadelphia. A number of English-speaking bishops had been invited to lunch at the Polish Hospice of St Stanislaus and there Tom met the Archbishop of Cracow, Cardinal Karol Wojtyla. He was a member of the Synod's permanent council and had been invited by Pope Paul VI to conduct the lenten retreat made by the Pope and the members of the curia the year before. A theological conservative and intellectual heavyweight, the cardinal was, nevertheless, a modest, humorous and friendly man. Tom took to him immediately and invited him to visit his fellow Poles in Scotland one day. Wojtyla seemed keen on the idea.

The following year, Tom Winning was appointed a member of the Congregation of the Doctrine of Faith, one of the dicasteries or departments of the Roman curia. At the Vatican Council there had been a demand for the internationalisation of the curia and it was decided that bishops from all parts of the world should be asked to serve as ordinary members of congregations for a period of five years. Tom had been asked to swell the ranks of the least popular department of church administration. The Congregation of the Doctrine of the Faith had formerly been known as The Holy Office. Its purpose was to safeguard Catholic doctrine and morals and clamp down on heresy. Its best known publication was the *Index of Forbidden Books,* a lengthy list of texts which Catholics were forbidden to read. For example, there was a time when a Catholic student, working for an honours degree in French at Glasgow University, had to obtain permission from his confessor to read a book by Rabelais, to meet the examination requirements. During Vatican II, the Holy Office was the subject of a great deal of discussion. It was agreed that its procedures were not adapted to the modern age and its censorious and repressive image did harm to the church.

Theologians and writers who had been 'silenced' because their work did not conform to the strict standards of orthodoxy laid down for their guidance, breathed a collective sigh of relief when, in 1965, Paul VI abolished the *Index of Forbidden Books.* From now on, no theologian was ever to be accused and condemned, but was to be heard and given a chance to correct what he had said or written. The old Holy Office was declared defunct. The Pope said that the defence of faith was better provided for by encouraging good theology. He appointed the Sacred Congregation of the Doctrine of Faith (CDF) to carry out a more positive function: 'to nurture and not to oppress, to reach out for the hearts and minds of the people.' There was to be a new emphasis placed on the positive promotion of wholesome doctrine rather than the condemnation of error alone. Questions in dispute were now to be thoroughly discussed during meetings of the congregation and decisions taken in plenary session. Would traditionalist watchdogs of the faith, set in the same mould as Cardinal Ottaviani, the apotheosis of Holy Office conservatism, be able to modify their approach to theologians whose writings had strayed from the path of orthodoxy? The Holy Office was the first department of the curia to be reformed, but on coming to his first meetings of the congregation thirteen years after it received its new constitution from Paul vi, Archbishop Tom Winning was to discover that some of the old attitudes were still firmly in place.

By inviting the Archbishop of Glasgow and other archbishops from around the world, the curia seemed to believe that this served to internationalise the congregation, but as these 'temporary' members were only invited to attend every two years, it seemed unlikely that they could make any valuable contribution to the work of the CDF. On his first visit to the former 'Holy Office', situated close to the Papal Audience Hall, Tom expressed his dissent with regard to what he described as 'lipservice' to the principle of internationalisation. The visiting bishops were given a resume of the congregation's work over two years only a short time before their three-day meeting. How could they possibly keep in touch with what was going on? The real decision-makers were obviously the cardinals in the congregation who were resident in Rome, headed by Franjo Seper, formerly the Archbishop of Zagreb and successor to Cardinal Ottaviani.

Not being fully *au fait* with the topics under discussion was bad enough, but the fact that the meetings of the CDF were conducted in Italian made matters worse. Tom felt that his fluency in the language was not what it had once been and during the *tour de table,* when each of the twenty members had to comment regarding the issues on the agenda, he felt himself at a great disadvantage. The South American bishops present were able to rattle away like native Italians, which seemed to add to his feelings of pressure. His difficulties were further compounded when Cardinal Baum, a non-Italian-speaking American, asked Tom to translate for him when it came his turn to speak.

Being in such a situation fairly concentrated the mind and, once he became used to the proceedings, Tom soon took the opportunity to comment and offer constructive criticism. Not all of his remarks found unanimous approval, however.

A favourite question for discussion during meetings of the Congregation was 'What shall we do with Hans Küng?' and it was the CDF's approach to this which confirmed Tom's belief that some

of the old Holy Office ways were still very much in force. Hans Küng
had been one of the theologians invited to speak in Glasgow during
the period when the Scottish Renewal Movement was in full flourish.
In books which he had written in the early seventies, Küng questioned the ordination of priests and the Vatican II definition of papal
infallibility. Küng held the view that there was no mention of a priesthood in the writing of St Paul and that only the power to pronounce
the words of consecration gave the priest superiority in relation to
other Catholics, but no right of leadership. Such a doctrine, if accepted,
would have a serious effect on vocations at a time when the church
was concerned at the small number of candidates coming forward for
the priesthood. Conservative theologians maintained that the *magisterium,* the teaching authority of the church, required obligatory
obedience. Küng, in the book entitled *Infallible,* was of the opinion
that unquestioning obedience could not reasonably be expected; the
theologians' role was to supply the magisterium with arguments and
evidence. Without them, this body would cease to exist. Presumably,
in pre-Vatican II days, books like *Infallible* would have been listed on
the *Index.* In the late seventies, the views of Küng and others were
beginning to cause some consternation among the conservatives, and
soon came to the attention of the CDF. Eventually, Hans Küng was
called to appear before the congregation to discuss some of his writings.
Tom Winning did not share Küng's views but it was the manner in
which the man was treated by the CDF to which he took exception.

First, he criticised members of the congregation for the period of
the year they had chosen to call Küng to Rome to give an account of
himself. 'Your public relations are abominable,' he told them, during
a *tour de table.* 'You attacked Küng and summoned him to Rome
when everyone else was writing their Christmas cards. Why couldn't
you have chosen a different time to do it?'

He told the congregation that it had been trying to sort out the
'Küng problem' for years without success and took it to task for not
permitting an advocate to come and support Küng when he appeared
before it. 'Even a man who's been charged with murder has a lawyer
to defend him,' said Tom. 'It doesn't matter who you are, you might
be the greatest theologian in the world but if you're not nervous and
upset at having been called to the highest point in the church to give
an account of yourself then you must be mad … Remember you're
innocent until you're proved guilty.'

Cardinal Seper said that it was in the regulations that individuals in Küng's position were not permitted an advocate to be present but Tom was not going to be put off by that reply. 'Who made the regulations? You made the regulations,' he told them and Cardinal Felici, the canon lawyer of the congregation, had to confirm that many, many years before, the Holy Office had allowed an advocate to defend a theologian 'on trial'.

Not all of the members present were impressed by Tom's challenging approach. Cardinal Benelli took particular exception to his outspokenness, calling him the *enfant terrible* of the group. However, Cardinal Willebrands congratulated him on demanding more justice for Küng. Tom himself felt only frustration with both their responses. He had little or no power to wield in the congregation: why then had it been down to him to bring more even-handedness into the situation?

At home, the press was starting to appreciate that the Archbishop of Glasgow, with his forthright manner, was definitely 'good copy'. As in Rome, not everyone agreed with his opinions; indeed for a church leader who was apparently very conservative, many of his statements caused a great deal of controversy. He had no hesitation in condemning what he considered to be the ills in society. In February of 1978, on being asked to inaugurate a War Memorial Chapel in his old school, Our Lady's High, Motherwell, he had some strong words to say. Reflecting on his own schooldays there and remembering his teachers who had gone to war, some to be killed in action, he asked: 'What did they die for? To get rid of the Nazis? Well, if that was the case why are we today adopting Nazi tactics, aborting people, sterilising them, just as those war criminals did?'

He also expressed concern about the nation's children: '... unless we see to the spiritual formation of our young people, as well as their intellectual and physical formation, we are in danger of becoming a nation of spiritual dwarfs, our spiritual life will be stunted.'

Nazis, dwarfs, such blatant language could not be ignored and when it was reported in the Scottish press, it served to irritate many who did not agree with his views and rouse the complacent within his own diocese. His unflinching determination to express what he believed and to defend the church was highlighted even more controversially in July of the same year when Tom Winning took the Prince of Wales to task for advocating a 'woolly' type of Christianity.

This situation arose after Pope Paul VI refused to grant a dispensation to Baroness Marie Christine von Reibnitz, a Catholic, and
Prince Michael of Kent, an Anglican, to be married in a Catholic
Church. Prince Charles, addressing a Salvation Army Congress in
Wembley shortly after this news broke, chose to make some remarks
which, although not specifically referring to the Pope or the royal
couple, were obviously alluding to them and the situation: 'When
people are uncertain about what is right and what is wrong,' the
Prince said, 'and anxious about being considered old fashioned, it
seems to be worse than folly that Christians are still arguing about
doctrinal matters which can only bring needless distress to a number
of people. Surely what we should worry about is whether they know
what is right and what is wrong or whether they are going to be given
an awareness of the things of the Spirit and of the infinite beauty of
nature; these are the things that matter.'

When the Archdiocesan Press Secretary, Rennie McOwan,
brought the report of the Prince's words to him, Tom Winning decided
that they demanded a response. Charles was obviously 'having a go' at
the Catholic Church. Both Tom and his Press Officer were sure that
whatever comments he, as Archbishop of Glasgow, might make,
would be forgotten almost immediately, buried under the welter of
responses from other sources, the hierarchy of England and Wales,
for example. Nevertheless, Tom issued a press release:

Prince Charles's statement presumably applied to the Pope's re-
fusal to grant a dispensation in relation to the marriage of Prince
Michael of Kent and Baroness Marie Christine von Reibnitz.

His remarks will cause annoyance and anger to millions of the
Queen's subjects who care deeply about doctrine and principle
and who also care deeply about relationships with fellow
Christians in other churches.

Perhaps he might care to enlarge his remarks to cover other
aspects of the case, such as the law of the land which prohibits
Roman Catholics from becoming monarch.

We all want to see relationships between the Christian churches
further improve, but it will not be achieved by papering over the
cracks and pretending that major differences of belief and practice do not exist.

To Tom's astonishment his words were not lost in the flurry of comments from other bishops; on the contrary he was the only member of the Catholic Church in Britain to speak out at all. In Scotland, England, Wales, the ecclesiastical silence was deafening. No one but Tom Winning dared to get involved at this level and his statement hit the headlines, the national TV, and travelled round the world like wildfire.

Letters poured into the archbishop's office and his home in Newlands, hundreds of them, mostly from English people. 'We are very loyal to the Royal Family,' was the most frequent comment, 'but we don't think Prince Charles had the right to say what he did ... it was inconsistent of him ...'

Charles had walked right into it and so, it seemed, had Tom. The phone rang continuously and extra help had to be brought in to deal with the calls. Months later, when English bishops (who had not dared to criticise the Prince) met Tom, they would say, 'We're glad you said that!' and he became quite a hero with Catholics as far afield as Australia. Sometime after the furore had subsided, Archbishop Justin Regali, an Italian American working in the Secretariat of State in Rome, confirmed that the Pope had been aware of the controversy from the newspapers. Paul VI was pleased that Tom had defended his decision not to grant the dispensation.

Although 'mixed' marriages had never been encouraged by the church, in recent years dispensations had been regularly forthcoming, provided both parties gave an understanding that any children of the marriage would be brought up as Catholics. During the period when Baroness Marie Christine's application for dispensation was being considered by the Pope and his bishops, she found it necessary to announce that any children of the marriage would be brought up as Anglican. Thus the Pope's hands were tied – to have agreed to a dispensation would have scandalised millions of Catholics throughout the world and confirm the suspicions of some that the church was more likely to bend the rules for those of rank and privilege than for ordinary people. The laws of the church had to be seen to be applied impartially, although by tradition, where Royalty was concerned, some additional consideration was always given and the Pope had the final word, perhaps to prevent a bishop being 'leaned on' by some powerful member of the nobility.

A further complication which prevented the Kents from being

married in the Anglican Church instead was that Marie Christine was a divorcee who had had her first marriage annulled by the Catholic Church. The Church of England does not recognise nullities, somewhat extraordinarily, since it owes its existence to a nullity taken by Henry VIII despite the church not granting it. Thus Prince Michael of Kent and the Baroness were married in a registry office in Vienna, followed by a very low-key church blessing in a small convent chapel. Marie Christine was said to have been very distressed by Pope Paul's decision, but some years later, Tom Winning was able to provide a happy postscript to the situation.

At the time of the marriage and in the prevailing situation, he had been against the granting of a dispensation but, when a reasonable period had elapsed, children born and the couple had 'tholed their assize', he knew that the marriage would become eligible to be considered for convalidation. Tom had kept in touch with the Apostolic Delegate, Archbishop Bruno Heim, regarding the subject and after a lapse of about five years, he advised the Delegate privately that the time had arrived when the situation could be reviewed. Heim was only too pleased to approach the English hierarchy again and put their recommendation before the Pope. As a result, the Royal marriage was convalidated at a ceremony held in the private chapel of Cardinal Basil Hume.

The Prince Charles controversy was soon eclipsed by other more dramatic events in the church. In August of 1978 Pope Paul VI died at the age of eighty and was succeeded by the Cardinal Patriarch of Venice, Albino Luciani. After only thirty-three days in office, the new Pope, who had taken the name of John Paul I, died suddenly of heart-failure. The world's cardinals had to travel back to Rome for a second conclave to choose another Pope. The result of their deliberations was stunning. The cardinals elected the first non-Italian Pope since the sixteenth century and the first to come from a communist country. The Archbishop of Cracow, the Polish Cardinal Karol Wojtyla became Pope John Paul II. How could Tom manage to persuade him to visit Scotland now? It was feasible for a cardinal to pay a call, but the Pope? That was the stuff of which dreams were made.

The Scottish bishops who attended both papal inaugurations were very pleased to have been joined on each occasion by the Moderator of the Church of Scotland for that year, Dr Peter Brodie, and the Reverend Donald McDonald, Principal Clerk of the Assembly. Tom was so touched by this that he wrote about it in the archdiocesan newspaper, *Flourish:*

> To travel to Rome twice in such a short space of time and during such a busy Moderatorial year was a magnificent gesture which the whole Catholic community in Scotland appreciates more than words can describe. Dr Brodie and the Reverend McDonald were our guests at the Scots College during their Roman visits and they endeared themselves to students and staff by their good humour, their friendliness and their desire to be as little trouble as possible.
>
> On the evening of Pope John Paul II's inaugural Mass, Dr Brodie, in a warm hearted speech, presented the college with a silver quaich as a momento of his visits and this personal touch moved many or us.
>
> The Rector decided to use the quaich as an open ciborium at college Masses as a constant reminder of these solemn moments and as a sign for all of us to pray for a continued growth in our relationship.

What with the euphoria engendered by the inauguration of a young Pope (at fifty-eight he was the youngest to be elected since Pius IX in 1846), the clear evidence of positive growth in the ecumenical movement and the new, at times controversial dynamism which Tom Winning had given to the Catholic image in Scotland, it seemed as if the decade was ending on an exciting and optimistic note. Glasgow's archbishop, however, had both feet planted firmly on the ground as usual. In 1979, he was writing in *Flourish:* 'I would not like to give anyone the idea that we are a complacent church.'

He was still worried about Mass attendance and the confusion which he felt sure had grown among Catholics after ten years of far-reaching changes in the church brought about by Vatican II. After discussion with Bishop Frank Thomson of Motherwell, he decided it was time to commission a scientifically conducted survey to carry out a Religious Poll on a national level, with the dioceses of Glasgow and Motherwell footing the bill of £70,000.

'That's not a lot for such a Poll in today's inflationary situation,' wrote Tom in *Flourish* of April 1979. 'Of course I feel it was worth it. Neither Bishop Thomson nor I would have invested that sort of money if we felt that it was unnecessary. If our first job is to improve the church and through it, the world, we must seek the realities of the present situation by the most sophisticated means available. As bishops and priests we are able to make reasonable predictions but they tend to be based on historical generalisations, as well, of course, as what we find in day-to-day visits around the dioceses. But our predictions lack the objective precision which a survey such as this secures.'

Of the nine hundred and eighty-nine Catholics interviewed in the poll, four hundred and fifty-seven were male and five hundred and thirty-two female. The interviewees ranged from age fifteen plus and came from varying social backgrounds. Among their number were married and single people, those in Catholic and mixed marriages. Seventy-nine were converts to the Catholic faith. A spokesman from Gallup, quoted in the April edition of *Flourish,* said: 'This is one of the most important and exciting investigations we have carried out and is the most sophisticated Catholic study done in the world.'

Certainly the results gave Tom Winning a clearer picture of the real nature of Catholic attitudes and practice and he published details of the poll, together with his own comments, in the archdiocesan newspaper. Anxious though he was about some of the findings, he was heartened that active concern for other people was considered to be one of the most important characteristics of being a Catholic and that eighty-two per cent of those interviewed agreed that praying regularly was vital. Even those who had not attended Mass for a year or more felt that the spiritual life was important Such positive attitudes could provide fertile ground for future pastoral development.

'We'll have to do more research to discover why they don't turn out at Mass,' was the archbishop's comment, 'but I can tell them with confidence, as Christ told Nicodemus: "You are not far from the Kingdom of God".'

Of those polled, only fifty-four per cent attended Mass on a weekly basis and the majority of those who had not been to Mass for more than a year did not consider their 'lapse' to be a serious sin. Some of the poll's results suggested there was a substantial body of 'non-practising' Catholics who would return to church-going if they understood their faith better. Further education seemed to be necessary for some of the regular church-goers too: when respondents commented on their belief in life after death, a puzzling uncertainty was highlighted. It would seem obvious that Catholics who go to weekly Mass and communion and who pray each day would have little hesitation in asserting the truth of as basic a statement as: 'There is life after death.' Yet one out of four who went to weekly Mass, one out of five weekly communicants and one out of four who prayed daily, believed that life after death was 'only probably true'. Perhaps the needs of Catholics like these would provide the greater pastoral challenge.

What relevance did religious practice really have for them? Was it not now an ingrained habit, an empty ritual? The church must surely be failing in the communication of its message as much for those people as for those who never attended church at all.

'I would be dishonest if I said I am not disturbed at the attitudes towards artificial birth control and divorce,' was Tom's response when the poll's findings showed only forty-six per cent disagreed with artificial contraception and fifty-eight per cent thought divorce should be allowed. 'The people interviewed were not moral theologians,' he observed, 'and I can understand how they are affected by society's attitudes towards these subjects. The church, internationally, has called divorce 'a plague' and it would be strange if our people were not to fall victims of that plague. I believe the poll results point towards the need for more communication among our people and more understanding, not just from the bishops and priests towards their flocks, but from the laity towards their spiritual leaders.' Paradoxically, over eighty per cent of those polled expressed a firm belief in the authority of the Pope – from whose magisterium the rulings concerning artificial contraception and divorce came.

The findings showed that the 'faithful' did not want their church playing party politics but believed that when issues that affect the freedom of everyone arise, such as abortion and euthanasia, the church should speak out. Responses to the sociological questions revealed that, largely, Catholics appeared to have overcome the 'immigration syndrome' and no longer felt like aliens in Scotland. Tom described this as 'a real breakthrough' and a 'tribute to our non-Catholic neighbours'. With eighty-nine per cent of the interviewees voting in favour of Christian unity, the effort to promote ecumenism had obviously paid off and *Flourish* readers were told that their archbishop would 'redouble his efforts' to promote unity among the churches.

One result about which all members of the hierarchy were particularly pleased was the seventy-three per cent support given to
Catholic schools. Tom Winning, who had been appointed Episcopal
President of the Catholic Education Commission the previous year,
had encountered a great deal of criticism for his advocacy of 'separate'
schooling, which seemed, to some, to contradict his ecumenical
stance. Catholic education was – and would continue to be – one of
the most contentious issues he had to deal with during his term of
office as archbishop. Criticism came from many individuals, such
bodies as the Church of Scotland, the Orange Lodge, the Educational
Institute of Scotland and members of Strathclyde Region's Education
Committee. Even some Catholics questioned the church's guardian-
ship of the rights granted to it by the 1918 Education Act: which
enabled Catholics to transfer their schools into the state system (after
forty-six years of paying both for Presbyterian national schools and
their own) while retaining their rights of teaching their own religion
and approving their own teachers.

Two months before the publication of the Gallup Poll results,
there had been such a flurry of critical comments that Tom Winning
had felt the necessity to respond in a full and frank way in the
columns of his archdiocesan newspaper:

… Many of these criticisms are expressed by well-intentioned,
caring people, including some Catholics, who are trying to weld
together different sectors of society, to end what they see as sectarian
tensions and to implement, they claim, a less expensive pattern of
Scottish education. There will always be, of course, isolated incid-
ences of less well-intentioned attacks when some critics want
Catholic schools ended simply because they fear the Roman
Catholic stand on Christianity or possibly out of envy because a
pattern of Christian teaching which was once implemented in
most schools is now largely confined to the Catholic sector.

It always seems to me that many of these comments are based on
a lack of understanding of the 'why' of our schools, the factors
that brought them into being, the state of religious education in
many non RC schools and the needs of society.

To us the gift of the Christian faith is a fantastic privilege to be
enjoyed, shared and passed on. It is an essential part of the shaping
of young people and the lives of all of us. To think of it an an

'optional extra' on the school timetable is to misunderstand totally
our position and attitude. Whatever the difficulties and inade-
quacies of how we handle RE within our schools, the fact remains
that it is still the best system at the present time for positively
teaching and passing on the sacred trust we have been given ... at
a time when Christianity is under attack, our land is being secularised and when the family unit and public spirited behaviour is
often sneered at. Scotland has always been proud of its Christian
heritage and our schools are part of that.'

He expressed disappointment that the Church of Scotland had
not resisted more strongly and more effectively the growing tendency
towards the removal of Christian education from Scottish schools.
'Individual ministers have told me that they could not in conscience
press us to join shared schooling so long as their own area of
Christian education was in its present uneven and downgraded state,'
he wrote. 'To many people, the idea of shared schools sounds a glowing
ecumenical target but in practice, it means replacing a firm pattern of
Christian teaching with nothing or with a few insipid periods of
watered-down religious education.'

He hoped that the independent Gallup Poll results would end,
for the foreseeable future, the constant niggle from some quarters
that Catholic parents were deeply divided on the schools' issue. 'The
parents stand by them in every respect,' was his comment, 'a real tribute to our Catholic teachers.'

He continued:

The terms 'segregation' and 'integration' are emotive because they
imply a removal of rights, the enforcing of bad laws as with the
South African policy of apartheid, whereas, in reality, in Scotland,
the law means that parents have a wider educational choice and
that you can send your child to a Roman Catholic school knowing
that positive attempts will be made to shape that child in the faith
in which we believe and to which we are committed.

So whatever plans Tom Winning would develop in the next
decade to improve the state of the church and promote interchurch
relations, giving up Catholic schools in order to 'integrate' with non-
denominational schools did not feature among them.

CHAPTER ELEVEN

The Papal Visit

Tom Winning's desire for a spiritual rejuvenation of the Catholic community, not just in his own archdiocese but in Scotland, was shared both by his fellow bishops and those in the church concerned that the faith now seemed to be irrelevant to the lives of a large number of people. The enormous potential to exert a more positive force in society which Catholics had was not being fully harnessed: the church was a sleeping giant needing to be awakened from its slumber. It was to receive a spiritual *reveille* at the beginning of the new decade.

The new Pope, John Paul II, was fast becoming a globe-trotter and within the first few years of his pontificate, had travelled more widely than any of his predecessors. He visited the Dominican Republic and Mexico, his homeland, Poland, the Republic of Ireland and the United States of America. In 1980, he visited Africa, France, Brazil and Germany. The Archbishop of Canterbury, Robert Runcie, wanted to invite him to Britain, however the Catholic bishops of England and Wales felt that such an invitation should come from them and at their conference they decided to go ahead and ask John Paul to come. 'Don't forget to ask the Scots,' said Archbishop O'Dwyer of Birmingham at that time. 'Of course not,' the other bishops said.

In August of 1980, Cardinal Hume of Westminster and Archbishop Worlock of Liverpool had an audience with the Pope, requesting that he visit the Catholics of England and Wales at a time suitable to him. The Pope could not give an immediate reply but appeared to welcome this invitation and sent the two prelates to see the Cardinal Secretary of State, Agostino Casaroli.

Casaroli said: 'What about the Scots? If the Holy Father is going to England and Wales, he'll have to go to Scotland as well.' 'We haven't asked them,' the English bishops replied. 'You'd better ask them, then,' was Casaroli's advice.

Cardinal Hume then phoned Cardinal Gray who, in turn, phoned all the Scottish bishops available at the time (it was the holiday season). The cardinal and the hierarchy were very happy to ask the Pope to visit Scotland and, a few days later, it was announced that the visit would take place during the early Summer of 1982.

Tom Winning was thrilled at the prospect; bringing the Pope to Scotland was not going to be so difficult after all. There was a buzz of anticipation throughout the Catholic community. Poles living in Scotland were particularly pleased. John Paul II was a hero to them and recently the archbishop had won the Poles' hearts entirely on account of the help he had given to Poland when martial law was proclaimed there and Solidarity came into existence.

He had joined forces with the Lord Provost of Glasgow and organised a campaign to raise money and send lorry loads of supplies to people in need in Poland. A show was put on at the Theatre Royal in Glasgow to raise more funds and the Italian tenor, Guiseppe de Stefano, drew a large audience. As a result of this, in 1980, Tom Winning was awarded a Polish decoration, the Order with Star of Komandoria Polonia Restituta, by representatives of 'the Polish Government in exile', who flew up from London to present him with the award at a ceremony in the Polish Club in Glasgow. He was told that he had given considerable help, both 'pastorally and spiritually' and befriended the Polish community in many ways. He had undoubtedly now become adept in persuading people to support what he believed were worthwhile causes. At this stage he did not know how useful his personal influence was going to be in bringing about the historic event for which the country had been given two years to prepare.

The bishops wondered if they could 'pull off' a papal visit with the same aplomb as the Irish in 1979, who had been given only fourteen weeks to get ready. A week before the Pope arrived in Ireland, a newspaper had reported confusion and chaos. In the event, it was a magnificent success and there was no one better than the Irish to advise the Scots on how to mount a similar exercise.

The visit had to be seen, not as an end in itself but as the starting point for a spiritual renewal. Preparations were to be aimed at changing attitudes rather than providing special religious services in the run-up to the Pope's arrival. The theme of the visit was to be 'Come, follow me!', general enough to allow John Paul to speak directly to his audience. A secondary theme, the objective of the spiritual preparation, was: 'Yes to God, Yes to life, Yes to each other!'

It was hoped that the visit would have an important ecumenical component and that the Pope could meet with the Moderator. 'Person to person contact does more for the course of Christian unity than many sessions of theological discussion,' said Bishop Thomson, who was responsible for the overall running of the visit. Of course there was a vocal minority who wanted 'No Popery' in Scotland and objected to John Paul's coming from the outset. Pastor Jack Glass of the Twentieth Century Reformation Movement was one of these, while members of the Orange Lodge and the Free Church of Scotland were also hostile to the visit. The bishops thought there could be troubles ahead. In Ireland, John Paul had said: 'Let no Irish Protestant think that the Pope is an enemy, a danger or a threat. My desire is that instead Protestants would see me as a friend and a brother in Christ.'

The Scots Catholics hoped that their Protestant countrymen would see the Pope in that way too.

Bishop Thomson appointed eleven committees, some five hundred people in all, to plan and organise the event. An itinerary was agreed and co-ordinated with the Bishops' Conference of England and Wales. Iona was given consideration as a starting-off point but was rejected due to the unpredictability of the weather in that area, even during June, and using helicopters. The arrangements were finalised eventually: arrival in Edinburgh, a Youth Rally at the Rugby Stadium, meeting with the Moderator and then with the priests and religious in the cathedral. Finally, on to Glasgow for an open-air Mass in Bellahouston Park.

It was the choice of the Bellahouston Park venue which, in Tom Winning's opinion, brought the anti-Papal feeling in Glasgow well into the open. He found the city's council leaders miserly in their treatment of the church, prior to the visit.

A request had been made by the church for some sycamore trees in the Park to be removed, because they would prevent an estimated thirty thousand people from actually seeing the Pope during the open-air Mass. As soon as news of this request was in the public domain, Glasgow, overnight, became a city of impassioned tree-lovers, with some people even lashing themselves to trees, as a sign of protest. The protest became personal and dangerous. The Scottish newspaper, *The Sunday Post,* received a phone call with the information that a large spruce tree in Archbishop Winning's front garden had been sawn three quarters of the way through its trunk, hence endangering both the archbishop and his property. The tree had to be cut down.

A delegation from the church went to the City Chambers and put the request to the city councillors again. They finally agreed that nine trees could be removed provided the church paid for them to be cared for in a nursery for two years. The final bill for this was £80,000.

The Director of Parks forbade the church to bring any lorries onto parts of Bellahouston Park unless they had balloon tyres. Tom Winning was extremely irritated to hear that when a recruiting campaign for the Army was held in the Park (some time after the church had received this edict), its trucks and lorries were allowed to move unhindered all over the grass. 'They didn't even get the Park railings painted!' he would be heard to say, after the event, disappointed that the city fathers, some of whom were Catholics, did not want to accommodate the church any more than was necessary.

Police in Edinburgh had no objection to the Pope travelling through the capital's streets but Strathclyde police saw things differently as far as Glasgow was concerned. Again Tom Winning was to be disappointed when the Chief Constable, Patrick Hamill, himself a Catholic, advised that, in order to avoid trouble with anti-papal demonstrators, who would undoubtedly turn up, the Pope should not be driven through the city's highways. Instead he was to be brought to Bellahouston by helicopter. The police undertook to give some form of training to the stewards who would help to control the people at the Mass. There would be thousands there.

Without a doubt, John Paul was a crowd-puller. It was not just that he was the first reigning Pope to set foot in Scotland, the leader of the world's Catholics – some seven hundred and fifty million people – he was, in himself, a charismatic figure, different from previous Popes. John Paul had a mystique about him, a strange kind of glamour. There was his Polish background for a start: his student days during the Nazi occupation of his country and later his fight against communism. His athletic prowess probably added more to his popular appeal than his formidable intellectual qualities. As Archbishop of

Cracow he had liked nothing better than to go skiing and climbing, and one of the first things he did on moving into the Vatican was to have a swimming pool installed to help keep him fit. No frail old Pope this, but a robust, strong man. His physical vigour and dynamic 'media' presence made him a most attractive personality. On pastoral visits he communicated powerfully with people in their own language, he laughed, joked, waved, shook hands, hugged babies. His sense of theatre was always to the fore: kissing the airport tarmac on his arrival in each new country was to become his trademark. Wherever he went, John Paul made an impact.

Tom Winning was anxious for the many parish groups to reach out to non-attenders to let them know they were welcome to 'Come and see the Pope.' Knocking on doors, house Masses, bulletins, the archdiocesan newspaper, were all used as means of communication. Pupils at Catholic schools were to be given the day off to see John Paul and each Secondary was responsible for making one set of priest's vestments for use during the huge concelebrated Mass. Technical classes began the production of ciboria (to hold communion hosts) in materials ranging from aluminium to ceramic. There was a buzz of excited anticipation throughout the country. However on 13 May 1981, it seemed as if the hopes and dreams of the Catholic community were about to be shattered. In St Peter's Square, while Pope John Paul was leaning out of his vehicle to shake hands with some of the many people attending his general audience, he was hit by two bullets fired at close range. He collapsed in terrible pain into the arms of his priest-secretary, was driven off at high speed back into the Vatican and then rushed by ambulance to the Gemelli Hospital in Rome. Death seemed near and he was given the Last Rites. Nearly six hours of surgery followed. The world was shocked. What kind of man would shoot the Pope? A young Turk, Ali Agca, had been arrested for the attempted assassination and everyone speculated as to who was behind the deed.

Relief came with reports that the Pope was still alive and responding to treatment. A message recorded in his hospital room was relayed to Sunday pilgrims at St Peter's, telling them that John Paul forgave the man who shot him and prayed for him. There seemed to be little hope, however, that the Pope would recover from his abdominal injuries to an extent that would enable him to resume his former active

life and visits overseas. Nevertheless, in Britain, people refused to believe that the Holy Father would not come to them in 1982 – in a
wheelchair, if necessary. They knew of his life as a young man and
were quite sure he was a survivor.

Thanks to the skill of surgeons and his own remarkable recuper-
ative powers, John Paul was back in his office at the Vatican by
October. Some said he would never leave it again. Many were anxious that he should stay there and avoid mingling with people and
putting his safety at risk. However, by February of 1982, John Paul
was off on his pastoral visitations again, this time to Nigeria, Benin,
Gabon and Equatorial Guinea. He was really back in harness! The
British Catholics heaved a sigh of relief and preparations for their
visit continued apace. But unexpected events which took place at the
beginning of April were to cast serious doubts once more as to
whether the Pope would come.

On 2 April, the Military Junta ruling Argentina invaded and
occupied the Falkland Islands with large army and naval forces. On 8
April, the British government, having initiated as many diplomatic
steps as possible, dispatched the first elements of a strong task force to
the assistance of the Falkland islanders, a journey of some eight thousand miles. More ships were to follow. The speed of the response had
been astonishing.

Two Christian countries likely to be at war, international relations
under intolerable strain. Would the Pope visit Britain in such circumstances? It seemed unlikely. How could he avoid alienating the countries
of South America with their Catholic populations?

As the days passed, there was no improvement in the situation.
Then ships were sunk, men were killed and wounded on both sides.
People said: 'The way things are, he can't possibly come!' But there
were others who countered: 'He must come at all costs!'

The voices of the latter group registered with Tom Winning. He
had no heart for contingency plans, though reason demanded that he
should think along those lines. To expect Catholics from all over
Scotland to come to a Mass in Bellahouston on 1 June, without the
Pope's presence, seemed to him to be unreasonable and he could not
accept this as a valid alternative.

Cardinal Gray and Cardinal Hume were invited to Rome for discussions. They returned in what was described as a 'mood of realistic

pessimism'. It seemed they were resigned to the fact that the visit would not go ahead if the war continued.

Tom Winning had come back from a meeting in Guernsey on Thursday, 13 May and went into his office the following morning feeling frustrated and helpless at this latest news. He felt he just had to do something. He spent the day phoning the other bishops and encouraging church groups to write or wire to the Holy Father pleading with him to come. He sent telegrams to the two Argentinian cardinals assuring them that the Pope's visit was to be pastoral, without state or political overtones. All the bishops agreed to put their names to a telegram to the Pope.

It was a long day, but in the evening, when Tom went home, he felt better – he had at least done something. However, when he phoned Gordon Gray to report his actions, the cardinal was less than pleased about the telegram to the Pope. After all, he had been out in Rome – Tom was flogging a dead horse! However, he came round, saying, 'All right, provided you abide by the Holy Father's decision.' Tom answered: 'That goes without saying,' knowing that the cardinal meant there was to be no fuss made if the decision went against them. The cardinal also recognised that the bishops had to give voice to their feelings.

On the morning of Saturday 15 May, Archbishop Worlock of Liverpool 'phoned Tom and said: 'What about the two of us going to Rome?' Tom said he would be pleased to go but also told the archbishop what had happened the previous day. 'I don't think Cardinal Gray would be too happy about it.' 'Well, I've cleared it with Cardinal Hume,' was Worlock's reply. When Tom Winning suggested it might be better if he got one of the other English archbishops to go with him, Derek Worlock did not agree. 'OK,' said Tom, 'I'll square it with Cardinal Gray.'

However, it was late on the evening of Sunday 16 May before he managed to track the cardinal down at what Tom called his 'bunker', a little cottage he had in Nunraw. 'If you want to go – go!' was Gray's crisp response on the telephone. 'But I'm going back to Edinburgh now. Can you come and see me there tonight?'

Tom arrived about midnight and they talked for hours as the cardinal brought him up to date on what had happened in Rome. Tom had arranged to leave from Turnhouse for Heathrow in the morning.

In London, Cardinal Hume had phoned the Vatican to say Archbishops Worlock and Winning were coming out to Rome for final consultations with the Pope – or the Secretary of State if an audience was not possible. When Tom and Derek Worlock arrived by different routes at Heathrow on the Monday morning, it was to discover two things: a message from Westminster archdiocese to say that the Holy Father expected both of them for lunch and that there was a strike at all the civil airports in Italy for the whole of that day!

The media had got wind of the fact that another attempt to bring the Pope to Britain was going to be made and there were TV cameras following the two bishops all over the place – first to Terminal 2 for the Alitalia Check-in desk and then, as they returned to Terminal 1, the cameramen walked backwards to record their progress. An airport official asked if they could walk along a corridor to be filmed again. 'Well,' said Tom Winning, 'on one condition: that you get us into the VIP lounge, because it looks as if we're going to be sitting here all day.'

By happy coincidence, one of the British Airways officials was of Polish origin and knew of Archbishop Worlock's connections with Poles in London. He was also keen to have a Polish Pope come to Britain. He arranged for the bishops to use the facilities of the hospitality room during the long hours of waiting. In the middle of the afternoon, he came to say that an Italian military aircraft had landed at the airport with an Italian general on board. Should he try to cadge the bishops a lift? They were not hopeful but readily agreed.

To their relief, permission was given by the Italian Embassy in London, allowing the two prelates to travel on the plane and it was about 5.00 p.m. when they eventually took off, accompanying the general on a direct flight to the commercial airport outside Rome, where only military aircraft were landing that day. Via Westminster, the bishops sent word ahead to Rome to say that they were on their way at last.

As he settled down on the plane, Tom thought of Cardinal Gray's words to him: 'The important thing is for the Pope to come and it doesn't matter who achieves it or makes it possible.'

During the flight, he wrote down thoughts and arguments related to the mission on which he and Archbishop Worlock were now engaged. He gave his notes the title 'The effects of non-arrival', and set them out in a list, as follows:

1. Bewilderment.

2. Catholics in Great Britain will be made to look ridiculous in the eyes of the world.

3. Confirmation of the Protestant belief that the Holy See is exerting pressure on the British Government to call off hostilities in the Falklands.

4. Withdrawal of credibility from all future Papal visits. No community can afford to invest its finances and expertise for an event which can be called off for unspecified reasons other than the physical impossibility of the Holy Father to make the visit.

5. We are now almost ready to receive the Pope. Over the years Scots Catholics have suffered for their faith. Is their courage to be rewarded with disappointment?

6. More than a million pounds has already been spent on Scotland. A cancelled visit would mean that this money has, effectively, been misused.

7. The lapsed have been encouraged to come back for this event. They would now be in a position to say: 'Does the Pope care about us?'

8. Ecumenism will be put back fifty years. The contact with Protestant leaders on their own ground will not take place. This opportunity may not be repeatable in our lifetime.

9. It may be said that the Pope was using the Falklands as an excuse to call off his visit because of some Protestant opposition to it.

10. The Papacy will not be regarded in the same way again in Britain.

11. If the Pope does not come, it will have an adverse effect on the position of the Catholic community in Scotland: some might ask, 'Do we count any longer?'

12. Yesterday, the Moderator of the Church of Scotland sent me a telegram saying: 'We in the Church of Scotland regard the Holy Father as a prophetic figure. If he doesn't come to Scotland, we will be sorry – he won't be a prophetic figure any more.'

When he concluded his note-taking it seemed no time at all until the plane touched down – it was certainly the quickest flight he had ever had to the Eternal City. He and Archbishop Worlock were met at the airport by the Scottish bishop, Agnellus Andrew, head of communications at the Vatican. Bishop Agnellus had a message from the Pope: John Paul understood the situation, would not expect to see the bishops that evening but looked forward to meeting them at lunch the following day. Tom had decided to stay at the English College which was fairly near the Vatican. This meant that he and Worlock could confer with the least inconvenience.

The following morning, Tuesday 18 May, the two bishops went to the secretariat which deals with Foreign Affairs where they found Monsignor Silvestrini most helpful. He suggested that they should link up with the Argentinians and make a statement together. Just before he joined the Pope for lunch, Tom met his Press officer, Father Tom Connelly, who had just arrived in Rome with Press Officers from England and Wales. Father Connelly had brought a copy of *Flourish* with him which was full of enthusiasm for the Papal visit. 'I'll take this to show the Pope,' said Tom, 'He has to come now if he reads this!'

Two Argentinian archbishops had been invited to join the papal lunch: Lopez Trujillo, whom Tom knew from working in the Congregation for the Doctrine of Faith, and Martinez Somallo, the Under-Secretary of State, who, when a student in the Spanish College, had been in Tom's theology class at the Gregorian University. Cardinal Casaroli, the Secretary of State, was the sixth member of the party, which, coincidentally, turned out to be a birthday celebration as well: John Paul was sixty-two that day.

The Pope started the discussions about the British visit as soon as the meal began. 'What language are we going to speak?' he said. Archbishop Worlock indicated that although he could not speak Italian, he did understand it, so Italian was the *lingua franca*. Tom decided he was going to eat as little as possible because he did not want to be found with his mouth full if he had something important to say. There was a lovely big birthday cake too!

The meal continued for two and a half hours whilst they worked out a package of different proposals. Archbishop Trujillo said quite bluntly that it would be a great pity if the Holy Father did not go to Britain but that he could not go in the present climate without giving great offence to the Argentinian Catholics. Trujillo was well aware that the conflict had begun as a result of Argentinian aggression, yet there was much popular support for the act and it had led to the present situation where there had arisen great antipathy between Britain and Argentina.

The purpose of this collegial initiative, the meeting of the Pope with these four bishops, became clear. It had to be an attempt to create the kind of climate in which it would be possible for the Pope to continue the visit without offending Argentina. Trujillo and Martinez were both of the opinion that the Argentinian cardinals, if convinced, could create this kind of climate, facilitating the visit to go ahead as planned. It would have to be demonstrated that the visit was essentially pastoral and in no way political, certainly not favouring one side or the other. The Argentinian cardinals would have to be helped to understand what the Pope's visit meant to the church in Britain and their support enlisted in conveying this to their own Catholic people.

Tom Winning presented the British point of view, using the arguments he had prepared on the flight to Rome. He also showed the Pope the telegram which he had received from the Moderator of the General Assembly which indicated that the Church of Scotland regarded the Pope as a prophetic figure. Tom asked John Paul if he would be prepared to go to Argentina after his visit to Britain. The Pope said 'Yes' without hesitation. In the end, that was how the crisis was resolved. However, at that stage there were a few things that had to be done before it could be said with certainty that the British Papal visit would go ahead. The Pope told the bishops to call back the cardinals for another meeting and tell them that there would be a Mass for Peace on the coming Saturday. Tom felt that things were going to work out favourably and later that evening some 'straight talking' with the Argentinian bishops helped to improve the general atmosphere even more. When he asked Lopez Trujillo directly, 'Why do you not want the Pope to come to Britain?' he answered, 'Oh anything the Pope wants, I want!' and a good discussion ensued.

Tom Winning had been impressed by the Pope's handling of the negotiations. With the exception of Cuba, each South American country had representatives of ambassadorial rank at the Vatican. Several cardinals who had worked in South America as nuncios, strong powerful types, had been getting at the Pope, saying that he risked alienating not only the people of Argentina but the rest of Latin America, who made up nearly half of the world's Catholic population. Thus he was under enormous pressure both politically and ecclesiastically, yet he did not succumb to the strength of their 'advice' but remained serene and objective. 'The church has got to rise above politics,' he said. Sir Mark Heath, the British Ambassador to the Holy See, said that the government was prepared to emphasise this fact by proposing that the planned meeting with the British Prime Minister should be removed from the Pope's schedule. If this helped the British Papal visit to go ahead then Mrs Thatcher had no objections. She had her own problems!

As a conclusion to the events of 18 May, Tom Winning and Derek Worlock issued a statement for general publication:

The Holy Father has confirmed his strong desire to make his Pastoral Visit to Great Britain. Conversations are continuing to see how present difficulties can be overcome.

Three days later, the archbishop again had lunch with the Pope and this time the cardinals were with them: Gordon Gray, Basil Hume, Ramul Primatesta of Cordoba and Juan Carlos de Aramburu of Buenos Aires. The South Americans, elderly men, seemed particularly tired after their journey and were quiet and subdued. The negotiations were long but finally agreement was reached and the Argentinians told the Pope, who had led the discussion, that they would do what he wanted them to do.

Subsequent to the lunch meeting, it was learned that British troops had re-landed in the Falklands, so the atmosphere on that Friday evening, when Archbishop Worlock was asked to draft a joint statement with his Argentinian opposite number, was inevitably strained. They achieved the task, however, 'for the love of the church'. The following day, at 7.00 a.m., the Mass for peace and reconciliation was due to be said in St Peter's Basilica. The morning started, not with solemnity and seriousness, but with an element of farce: the water in the college where Archbishops Winning and Worlock were staying had been cut off. They had to rush round, trying to get a wash and shave, in order to get to St Peter's in time for this major liturgical event.

The Pope, the cardinals and the bishops who had worked on the negotiations celebrated the Mass. There were also British and Argentinian seminarians present and a sizeable contingent of the British community in Rome. There was still some tension underlying the public reconciliation amongst the celebrants but, when the Mass was over and they had heard the Pope quote from St Augustine that the highest title to glory is 'to kill war with the words of negotiation, instead of killing men with the sword', it seemed inevitable that the visit would go ahead. After the Mass, the prelates went their own way. Tom, with the Rector of the Scots College, Father James Clancy, walked to a cafe near the college to get some breakfast and then on to see an old lady he knew who stayed close by. Only half an hour had elapsed when, on his return to the college, he was met by an anxious member of staff hurrying to meet him. 'You've got to go back to the Vatican!' he was told, 'Cardinal Gray's gone already!'

What had happened now? Tom got there as fast as he could. Fortunately for him, the Pope was giving an audience to President Mugabe of Zimbabwe, and appointments were running late, so he made it in time. It was not John Paul the bishops were to see, however, they had been summoned by Cardinal Casaroli, the Secretary of State.

There was something in Casaroli's manner, as he addressed them that morning, which reminded Tom of one of his more formidable teachers at Our Lady's High School. 'I want to restate what was said yesterday,' Casaroli informed the four prelates, 'that the responsibility for the Pope coming to Britain will be yours and you will have to decide whether, under the circumstances, it is right for him to come or not.'

Feeling rather like recalcitrant schoolboys, the bishops could only say yes, of course they accepted responsibility. Obviously the cardinal was concerned about the Pope's safety. The Vatican had received some intelligence from the French Foreign Office indicating that one of the bridges in London was going to be loaded with explosives. What if a disaster like that happened when John Paul was in Britain?

Finally, Casaroli dismissed the bishops, leaving them on a rather off-key note. Worlock, whom Tom regarded as a 'great operator', decided to stay on in Rome, telling the others: 'You never know what might happen!' Tom felt sure that, no matter what red tape Casaroli tried to wind round the situation, the Pope would still come to Britain and he and the two cardinals went home.

The rest of that weekend and the morning of Monday 24 May were difficult for Archbishop Worlock because of the situation in the Falklands and news of severe fighting going on. The curia still gave the impression that the Pope might not come to Britain at all. However, after lunch on the 24th, it became clear to Worlock that if he could introduce the question afresh, without any reference to what had taken place the previous week, it would be dealt with as a new issue. This meant the rapid preparation of still more memoranda merely asking for confirmation that the Holy Father would come the following Friday for a pastoral visit. At 5.30 p.m., whilst waiting in the Secretariat of State, Worlock received the answer that the Pope would be arriving at Gatwick on the following Friday. The Archbishop of Liverpool left Rome immediately that night, so the matter could not be re-opened. He announced that the visit was definitely 'on' as soon as he landed in Britain.

So it was on 28 May 1982 that John Paul II arrived by Alitalia jet at Gatwick Airport, the first Pope in history to set foot on British soil. Cardinal Hume and the Duke of Norfolk, representing the Queen, were there to greet him, together with various dignitaries, both lay and ecclesiastic. Tom Winning was among the latter group and the Pope, with a quizzical smile, said to him: 'This is England! I'm not in Scotland yet!' To which Tom answered: 'Yes, but I just had to come to welcome you!' Father Stanislaw, the Pope's secretary, knew what Tom was thinking and announced with a grin: 'We are here!' Tom's reply was a barely audible but nevertheless fervent: 'Thank God for that!'

Among the Papal entourage was an old friend of Tom's from his days as a canon law student in Rome, Paul Marcinkus, now an archbishop and personal bodyguard to Pope John Paul during his overseas visits. British policemen had also been assigned to protect the Holy Father.

The first Mass of the British pastoral visit was in Westminster Cathedral at which were present the bishops of England and Wales and representatives of the Anglican, Orthodox and Free Churches. This was followed by a visit to Buckingham Palace where the Pope had a private meeting with the Queen. Then it was on to St George's Cathedral in Southwark in which the Pope anointed a number of very sick, elderly and handicapped people. Back at Westminster he addressed the hierarchy of England and Wales, the last engagement of day one of the visit.

On the following morning, John Paul went to Roehampton to speak to a large gathering of Catholic and Anglican religious. A helicopter flight then took him to Canterbury where he met Prince Charles before taking part in a special service with Robert Runcie, the Archbishop of Canterbury. In ecumenical terms, this was the most significant event of the English visit: the Pope and the archbishop, in the Deanery, signed a declaration which recognised the steps which the Catholic and Anglican communions had taken along the road to unity and outlining the hopes and plans they shared for 'the next stage' of their 'common pilgrimage'. After kneeling in prayer with Dr Runcie at the site of the martyrdom of St Thomas Beckett, the Pope met with members of the British Council of Churches. Then he left Canterbury, once more by helicopter, going to a Mass attended by eighty-thousand people at Wembley Stadium.

The next day, Pentecost Sunday, the Pope met his fellow country-men – some four thousand Poles – at Crystal Palace Sports Centre, and then he celebrated Mass at Coventry Airport for a massive gath-ering of 350,000 people. The pace of the visit did not flag; by the afternoon the Pope was in Liverpool where he travelled through Toxteth, taking part in a Service at the Anglican Cathedral before being welcomed at the Cathedral of Christ the King by Archbishop Derek Worlock, for another Mass. The Pope stayed at the archbishop's house that night as there was another busy schedule lined up for the following day.

31 May dawned, bright and sunny. The Pope started the day's pro-gramme by meeting with Sir Immanuel Jakobovits, the Chief Rabbi of the United Kingdom and the Commonwealth, and other leaders of the Jewish community, at a convent in Manchester, before saying Mass at Heaton Park, during which twelve men were ordained to the priesthood. The final event of the English visit was held at Knavesmire Racecourse in York where thousands of couples renewed their marriage vows. Then the Pope flew to RAF Turnhouse in Edinburgh. He had arrived in Scotland at last!

Cardinal Gray and the Scottish hierarchy were there to meet him, as, in his by now customary way, he knelt to kiss the ground of Scotland.

Familiar though he was to receiving an enthusiastic greeting in the different countries he had visited, even John Paul was not prepared for the exuberant welcome he was given at Murrayfield Stadium in Edinburgh, his first stop on the Scottish visit. There Cardinal Gray announced to him: 'Dear Holy Father, I bring you the young Catholics of Scotland!'

Over forty thousand of them, off school for the day, cheered, applauded and sang to the Pope with uninhibited emotion, holding up his address with their fervour. There were those who, later on, criticised the young people's behaviour, saying that the chants of 'John Paul, John Paul' and the chorus of 'You'll never walk alone' were more appropriate at a football match. The Pope, however, absolutely loved it. He tried to calm them: 'Basta!' he said in Italian. 'Enough!' At one point, as he stood on the dais, flanked by the Scottish hierarchy and waiting to continue his speech, he turned, caught Tom Winning's eye and burst into hearty laughter. There was no doubt that the Scots appreciated his coming.

'Dear young people of Scotland,' he said to them. 'Thank you for your welcome, for the words and for the song. I am happy that my first contact is with you, the pride of your beloved country and the promise of its bright future...'

If the so-far highly demanding pace of the British visit had caused the Pope's energy levels to flag, he certainly had them replenished by the highly charged atmosphere of Murrayfield.

The next stop was, by contrast, brief and restrained but no less significant. In the forecourt of the Church of Scotland Assembly Hall, John Paul met Professor John McIntyre, the Moderator, who told him that the national church looked forward to further dialogue with the Catholic Church: '... not only on topics of disagreement but also on joint themes on which we agree.'

The statue of John Knox, he who, four hundred years before, had been zealous in his efforts to stamp out 'popery' in Scotland, overlooked the scene. More than a few present must have wondered what he would have made of this reconciliation. Some anti-papal protesters waved their banners at John Paul as the 'popemobile' progressed through Princes Street, but he succeeded in disarming the group by turning round and giving it his blessing.

After meeting the Scottish clergy and religious in St Mary's Cathedral, the first day of the Pope's visit to Scotland was complete. On the morning of 1 June, John Paul had a private meeting with the Moderator in Cardinal Gray's residence and later he spoke to a number of other Scottish church leaders. After this, he went to a hospital for the severely handicapped in Rosewell to speak to the residents and staff. Then it was over to the West of Scotland. Here Tom Winning introduced him to students and teachers from throughout the country who had gathered at the National Catholic Teachers' Training College, St Andrew's, Bearsden, in Glasgow.

The highlight of the Scottish visit was the Mass held at Bellahouston Park, the venue around which there had been so much controversy. Some three hundred thousand people gathered to greet the Pope, while in another part of the city's south side, police kept guard outside Tom Winning's home. He was taking no chances, after the tree incident. He felt relaxed and happy though, as he listened to the Pope speaking in the brilliant sunshine and reminding the Scots Catholics of the efforts made by their ancestors to keep the Catholic faith alive when it was in danger of becoming extinct.

'Dear beloved Catholics of Scotland,' he addressed them. 'The prayers of your forefathers did not go unanswered ... with grateful hearts turn to God and thank him that tranquil days have been restored to the Catholic community in Scotland. ... What was a dream a century ago has become the reality of today. A complete transformation of Catholic life has come about in Scotland with Catholics assuming their legitimate role in every sector of public life ...'

The Pope also acknowledged that there were still difficulties which they had to deal with today: 'The spirit of the world would have us capitulate on the most fundamental principles of our Christian life ... I assure you, we are acutely aware of the problems you have to face.'

'You originate in a glorious past,' said the Pope, 'but you do not live in the past. You belong to the present and your generation must not be content simply to rest on the laurels won by your grandparents and great-grandparents. You must give your response to Christ's call to follow him.'

The welcome John Paul received at Bellahouston was nothing short of rapturous: he had to pause in his homily for eight minutes to allow the crowds to give vent to their enthusiasm. At last, after all the brouhaha before the visit – was it on, or wasn't it? – he had come to see them. The shouts and cheers were of relief. At last, the Catholic community, the biggest religious minority in Scotland, had come of age: its very own Pope had come to their country to affirm it. The shouts and cheers were of pride. As Tom accompanied the Pope on the Papal transport for a tour round the park after Mass, his grin was one of triumphant delight. Surely this was the very thing the church needed to revitalise it?

When John Paul prepared to leave in the helicopter which had

brought him to Glasgow from Edinburgh, the crowds realised the
visit was over, the cheering would soon stop and that there were no
more hymns to be sung. But the voices rose in a final accolade to the
Pope, quietly at first, then gaining in strength and volume:

Wull ye no cam' back again?
Wull ye no cam' back again?
Better lo'ed ye canna be,
Wull ye no cam' back again?

John Paul, recognising the feeling and poignancy in the melody,
turned to Tom and asked: 'What is that song?' 'Holiness, it's a song of
farewell,' Tom explained, 'saying you are well-loved and asking you
to come back to Scotland again. It was written originally for Bonnie
Prince Charlie.' The Pope looked slightly baffled and thought about
this for a moment. Then his face cleared. 'Ah yes!' he said, 'I was talking to him in Canterbury just a few days ago!'

The last part of the British pastoral visit, on 2 June, was spent in
Wales, with Mass and a youth event in Cardiff. The weather had
broken but spirits were still high as John Paul took his leave of the
Catholic community in Britain:

It is my hope today, as I return to Rome, that you will remember
why I came among you. And as long as the memory of this visit
lasts, may it be recorded that I, John Paul ii, came to Britain to
call you to Christ, to invite you to pray!

So, the six-day event had come to an end. The Pope had preached
– what seemed like thousands of words – in his usual uncompromising way. He had said Mass, blessed the sick, baptised, confirmed, ordained and travelled all over the country at a remarkable pace. He
had laughed and joked. No pop star could have aroused more enthusiasm. He left in his wake a great surge of euphoria. The question
was: would it last?

All the Scottish bishops had agreed, prior to the visit, that it was
never to be seen as an end in itself but as a catalyst for a complete renewal process. The church seemed to have 'come alive' as it had never
done before during this unique event and there was a feeling that
people had experienced something of the vision that was spoken of at
Vatican ii, the vision to reflect all the warmth and strength of community that was so characteristic of the early church. Tom Winning was
the first to capitalise upon this experience, to use it as a preliminary

step leading to a renewal of faith in the archdiocese. The following year, 1982, he set out his plans for the future of the church in Glasgow, plans which had been taking shape in his mind since the sixties. Bringing the Pope to Scotland was a remarkable feat, but trying to change attitudes in his own church community? That was a challenge of quite a different order, altogether.

CHAPTER TWELVE

The Pastoral Plan

On subsequent occasions, when Tom Winning met the Pope in Rome, John Paul would invariably say: 'Ah! Bellahouston! I have it all here...' and pat his heart. The reception he had been given in Scotland was the warmest he had ever enjoyed – outside of Poland. Certainly, Scottish Catholics' loyalty to their Pontiff could never be questioned, nor their respect for 'the priest', nor their generosity of spirit in response to those in need. Nevertheless, certain unwelcome facts still had to be faced: up to sixty per cent of Catholics did not attend church – and the figure was continuing to grow. Despite the pre-papal visit 'reach-out', the church in Glasgow had lost contact with many people.

Tom Winning saw that the first group which needed help and re-quired to be given an appetite for renewal was the clergy. He set up the 'Ministry to Priests', inviting Brother Loughlan Schofield from the United States to offer a course for Glasgow priests, enabling them to consider their ministry. When asked to identify what their experience of priesthood had been, at the initial meeting some of the responses were revealing:

'I don't know when I last conducted an entirely Catholic marriage or baptised a child of two Catholic parents ...'

'I visit the homes of parishioners and nobody even turns off the television ...'

'You go out on Sunday for Mass and do your best and, Sunday by Sunday, there are fewer people there ...'

At the end, Brother Loughlan Schofield told the priests that many of them were suffering from a classic case of 'burn-out', their job satisfaction was nil, a situation fast becoming common in the Western church. It wasn't the men in huge parishes in Africa, with no material security, who were prime cases for heart attacks. Their enor-mous churches were too small for the number of parishioners, and their ministries gave them tremendous satisfaction. It was a different matter for priests in Glasgow who might look at their parish records and say, 'I've got two thousand on my books and only five hundred at Mass. I must be failing my people in some way.'

To care for the carers first had to be a priority and one hundred and seventy-two priests in the archdiocese took part in the 'Ministry' programme designed to deal with their spiritual, psychological and intellectual growth. Support groups were set up and soon priests were finding themselves engaged in counselling their fellow priests. It was a novel development.

Tom Winning had renewed his connections with the 'Movement for a Better World' at a course in Malpas in Cheshire and felt that it might be able to give him the help he required. After having a meeting with the religious of the archdiocese, his ideas began to crystallise. He invited a Jesuit, Father Max Taggi, from the Better World Headquarters in Rome, to visit the archdiocese. Max Taggi had a reputation for helping dioceses plan for the future and was known internationally as a 'trouble-shooter' in diocesan terms. From him, Tom Winning required advice on helping the diocese look at its situation following the Pope's visit, how to build on the good things that emerged from it and respond to the challenge of it. This would involve radical change, if the church was to make progress.

Over a period of seven days, the three bishops, the vicar general and the vicars episcopal considered every aspect of church life and recorded the various strengths and weaknesses. They concluded that there was insufficient co-ordination in the diocesan efforts to reach certain people and that a 'pre-pastoral plan' was probably necessary.

Max Taggi helped Tom Winning work out a pre-pastoral programme for the next three years. He laid down four general objectives:

The church in Glasgow had to:

1. become more aware of its mission.

2. promote partnership and co-responsibility.

3. encourage human and spiritual formation of every individual in the church – clergy and laity – to equip them to become partners in the life of the church.

4. renew structures in the church to bring this about.

The archbishop put this in the following way: 'It means moving from a 'pray, pay and obey' kind of church to one which is more concerned about unity within community and harnessing the gifts with which we are all blessed.'

To oversee the plan, a Central Promoting Team was appointed. In addition to the archbishop and his two auxiliaries, it comprised Fathers Richard Dunne, Colman McGrath and Hugh McEwan, Sister Mary Kilday, Nicola Lynch and Dorothea Sweeney, Dr Anna Murphy and Mr Pat Reilly.

Father Hugh McEwan (not the same man who was ordained alongside Tom Winning) was appointed as Co-ordinator of the plan and as Director of the Pastoral Centre, which was established in premises taken over from Nazareth House, Cardonald.

Tom Winning's 'new ideas' were not welcomed wholeheartedly by either priests or people. Considerable inertia had to be overcome. When meetings were held of priests, religious and lay people, there were difficulties: some priests did not like the idea of consulting with the laity, while some lay people found it difficult to speak as 'equals' to their priests. Nevertheless, the work put into this early stage was immense. A large group of committed Catholics was asked to define its vision of the church in the 1990s and certain underlying anxieties emerged: priests talked of the need for co-operation between priests and bishops; religious spoke of the need for the church to be seen going out to others; laity felt there was a need for more education on Vatican II; continually, reference was made to the 'missing youth'.

This group was formed into a Resource Team and trained at the Pastoral Centre to go out to 'pilot' parishes and tell them about the idea of pastoral planning. A number of difficulties arose because not everyone was a good communicator and the approach which some members of the team adopted showed their lack of experience. In addition, there were those parishioners who resented other lay people talking to them about the church. However, the parish meetings helped Tom and his team find out what people were saying and thinking and what vision of the church of the future they had. Getting people to change to a 'new' vision of the church was an uphill task, and many felt that their own parishes needed a strong injection of spirituality if they were to do this and find a way of reaching out to people who were not going to church.

In response to this, Tom Winning went to Newark, New Jersey, to find out more about a spiritual programme entitled 'Renew' and he invited Monsignor Tom Kleissler and Sister Donna Ciangio from the Renew Central Office to visit the archdiocese. The programme involved Catholics coming together in their neighbourhoods to read and discuss scripture: special events, both spiritual and social, were organised in the parishes and a messenger system set up for the delivery of parish newsletters to inform everyone, practising Catholics or not, of what was happening. The programme seemed to have potential. However, as the Central Promoting Team considered whether it should be included in the plan, changes in direction started to take place which were to lead to a crisis.

Father Max Taggi, returning to Glasgow from Rome to evaluate the archdiocese's progress, announced that he was being sent out East by his Jesuit superiors. In September 1985, therefore, the position of facilitator was taken over by Father Juan Baptista Cappellaro, an Argentinian priest, who was based in Rome. He had worked with Father Lombardi, the founder of the Better World Movement and had been heavily involved in the business of pastoral planning. Over a period of twenty years, Father Cappellaro had tested out his theories in a parish in Italy. He asked for two studies to be made in time for his arrival in Glasgow: a detailed analysis of the social, economic and religious background of the city and its people and a history of the archdiocese, identifying causes of the church's present situation. A review of the documents produced served to confirm what Tom Winning had already known: that there were parts of Glasgow where Catholics living in deprived areas had a sense of hopelessness which prevented them from seeing the church as significant in their lives. All the priests of the archdiocese had access to the studies and, although there were positive aspects, the overall results made bleak reading. The clergy was upset: everyone had thought that Glasgow was such a wonderful place, at least in comparison to many others, and here it was – in church terms – deteriorating year by year.

The archbishop tried to get across to the priests that the spirituality of the pastoral plan, the spirituality of change, was that they should take ownership of the reality. 'Don't blame yourselves for the results of the analysis of the archdiocese,' he told them. 'If there's any blame, then everybody's to blame. That's not the point, the point is to remedy it!'

The members of the Resource Team – the lay people who had done a great deal of work visiting the 'pilot' parishes – were also unhappy. Cappellaro advocated fundamental changes in the implementation of the plan. It would have to be recognised, he said, that the business of pastoral renewal would be a long, slow process gradually becoming all-inclusive; from this point on it was necessary to have the whole diocese move forward under the leadership of the priests in the parishes. So the idea of 'pilot' parishes was to be dropped: the church of Glasgow must move as a whole, or not at all. A 'Deanery Animating Team', made up of people from the Deaneries, was selected to replace the Resource Team, which was told that its services were no longer required. Puzzled as to why the teams could not simply be re-arranged, and hurt that their contribution seemed to be undervalued, a number of lay people began to feel 'turned off' by the whole idea of pastoral planning.

Meanwhile, it was decided that the archdiocese should adopt the American 'Renew' Programme to give the parishes a new spiritual dimension. When the first session of 'Renew' began in October 1985, one hundred and three parishes were actively involved with some fifteen thousand people engaged in scripture-sharing groups throughout the city. In those parishes which took part, there was a real spiritual 'high' at the end of the week's renewal retreat, but the maintenance of that spirituality depended on how the priests of the parish saw the whole pastoral plan. Was it just another organisation or was it something really new and all-encompassing, taking over the parish? Tom Winning's vision of it was that it should colour everything, the whole life of the parish, but he had not yet successfully transmitted this idea to the clergy. When the 'Deanery Animating Teams' went back to parishes some months later, to give a 'refresher' retreat and assess what had transpired, they found in some cases that the momentum had sagged because the parish priest had not taken ownership of it. Some priests would say, 'If the archbishop wants to do this, I won't stand in his way!' In reality, many of them were tired of meetings, meetings and more meetings. Did they not have enough to do?

Their archbishop was, in fact, moving much too fast, something which his friend Bishop Donny Renfrew had no hesitation in pointing out to him. 'You can't expect everyone to have the same vision as yourself,' Donny would say, 'Give them time!'

So now Tom Winning found himself in a lonely and difficult situation. Here he was, trying to launch a pastoral plan when no other bishop in the country was doing so. Perhaps he was sticking his neck out too far? Already it could be seen that he was running the risk of losing much in terms of his standing with his own clergy if the plan failed to take off. Yet he also knew that when you try to change people, particularly in the church, you will always meet resistance. Vatican II was a prime example. There was always pain in change.

A visit to missionaries from Glasgow working in Peru, Bolivia, Argentina, Brazil and Ecuador gave Tom a deeper conviction that he would be failing the church if he did not try to solve the problem of Catholics not attending Mass. When he saw for himself the obstacles the church in Latin America had to face and yet it was forging ahead of its European counterpart in combatting spiritual and material poverty, he was sure that the problems he was facing could be overcome.

It was not simply to be a matter of a parish priest trying to 'service' an area as in previous times. Tom wanted the parishes of the archdiocese to be divided into neighbourhood groups so that all Catholics, whether they went to church or not, could engage in prayer and study of the gospels in order to instil Christian virtues in their own community. He wanted people in the same street to talk to one another and so encourage non-attenders to 'come back'.

The Belgian Cardinal Suenens once said: 'Blessed are those who dream dreams and have the courage to pay the price of them.' Archbishop Winning had a dream for sure, and equally surely had to pay the price of it. He still had to convince his priests that his dream could become a workable reality and was not the threat it appeared to be. His immediate priority was to shorten the psychological distance which had grown between the clergy and himself in order to improve relationships. He met with them in groups of fifteen, spending a day with each group, discussing the plan, the role of the priest in it and celebrating Mass with them. It was an arduous time for him.

The lay people who had been quite unnecessarily alienated were largely persuaded that it was lack of expertise on the part of the Central Promoting Team which had caused a breakdown in communication. By 1988, the directorate of the pastoral programme was changed, with Tom deciding to appoint four priests and one religious to devote all their time to the pastoral programme. His rationale for this was, if he could afford to have eight men working full time to train twenty students for the priesthood in the seminary, he should have no qualms in appointing four to help implement the plan for three hundred thousand Catholics.

New structures were created at parish, deanery and diocesan level which facilitated participation and gave priests and people a chance to have their say.

Gradually, by the end of the eighties, those who had thought the plan would simply 'go down the drain' without the archbishop there to galvanise it, became aware that the archdiocese was indeed beginning to embrace the plan. It had taken since 1982 for the church to get to the stage where eighty per cent of the parishes had their own co-ordinating team in some shape or form, with varying degrees of strength and success. There was, at last, an acceptance that such teams should be in place and a realisation that if the church were to survive, the old ways of doing things had to change.

In a pastoral letter in 1989, Tom Winning wrote: 'Trust my leadership! I have made the spiritual renewal of Glasgow my life's work...' It seemed at last that the priests and people were now prepared to acknowledge that their archbishop's reading of the signs of the times was accurate and that, if they followed his direction, they would be in safe hands.

Whilst the eighties were dominated by the setting up of the pastoral plan, a number of other significant events took place during this period. The city and the country honoured Tom Winning in several ways. In 1983 he was awarded the Loving Cup, the city of Glasgow's special award for outstanding service, in recognition for the part he played in bringing Pope John Paul to Scotland. In the same year, the University of Glasgow conferred on him an Honorary Doctorate in Divinity. Professor Peter Walsh of the Humanities Department, in his address at the ceremony, referred to the fact that Tom Winning's leadership had been extended not only to the spiritual health of his own flock but also to promoting greater civic responsibility and readier co-operation with other churches. 'The hoary joke that at Parkhead the Old Firm teams now emerge to the cry: "Get stuck into our separated brethren" may contain a germ of poetic truth', said the Professor to appreciative laughter throughout the Bute Hall. Reference was also made to the discussions then in progress regarding the feasibility of students for the priesthood taking part of their training at the university and to the archbishop's enthusiastic support for this proposal.

This was a good spirited occasion: newspaper photographers captured the jocular mood with pictures of Tom, Alistair Maclean, the Scottish novelist now Doctor of Letters, Hamish MacInnes the mountaineer now Doctor of Laws and the other newly appointed 'Doctors' larking around in the university quadrangle with musical instruments. Some rather off-key notes were sounded, however, at a later date, when it was proposed by Motherwell District Council that Ritchie Street in Craigneuk in Wishaw be renamed Winning Quadrant in honour of a local boy who had: 'reached the top of his chosen profession'. Wishaw True Blues Loyal Orange Lodge Number 208 took grave exception to this, believing a local footballer and a local boxer were more appropriate choices than a Catholic bishop. In a letter of protest to the Council, the Lodge's secretary wrote: 'We feel that Tommy Gemmell and Chic Calderwood were great ambassadors for Craigneuk. Their only allegiance was dedication to their respective sport, whereas Archbishop Winning's total allegiance belongs to a city called Rome.' The Councillor James Foley, who proposed changing the name of the street, replied by saying that if Tom Winning had become Moderator of the Church of Scotland, he would have been just as happy to see a street named after him. 'Professor William Barclay, a famous Church of Scotland member, was born in Motherwell and we have already named a street in his honour,' said Foley and so Winning Quadrant came into being, despite the Lodge's protest. Tom Winning was flattered but the objection was a blunt reminder, if he needed one, that religious sectarianism was alive and well and still flourishing in Scotland.

He also received the Glasgow Lord Provost's Medal, and in 1986, the Educational Institute of Scotland, the largest of the teachers' unions, awarded him an Honorary Fellowship. That it was offered and that it was accepted was generally greeted with surprise. The previous year, during the middle of the teachers' pay dispute (1985-86), Tom's relations with the EIS became strained, to say the least, when the subject of Catholic schools was raised, yet again.

One Mr K. McLachlan, retiring President of the EIS, said in his farewell address to the 1985 Conference: 'The segregation of children only five years old on religious grounds is wrong and grossly so ... in this matter the law is not merely an ass but an assassin ... it is a deliberate arrangement of our society, codified by statute ... the law of the land ... which dictates that our children do not enjoy socialisation and education together, as they should ...'

Doughty as ever, when it came to fighting his corner, Tom Winning replied to this, through the press: 'Let Mr McLachlan put his own house in order and bring the strike to an end. He is talking utter rubbish and I have no time for him or the EIS. It shows what the Catholic community has to put up with from people who, I believe, have no time for religion in schools.'

Following the 1918 Education Act, the Catholic Teachers' Federation joined the EIS only after being given a 'gentlemen's agreement' that its schools would be respected. This was not the first time that members of the EIS had attempted to undermine the position of Catholic schools. However, despite his supreme irritation with the union, Tom and members from other churches played an important role as middle men between the teachers and the government and contributed to the settlement of the dispute. Perhaps the offer of the Honorary Fellowship was an olive branch extended to the Archbishop of Glasgow for services rendered. He accepted it in that spirit.

Progress continued to be made to some extent in the area of church unity. At Pentecost, in 1984, the Iona Community invited Scotland's church leaders and members of various denominations for a two-day programme of prayer, discussion and community living on the island. Representatives from the Church of Scotland, the Episcopal, Baptist, Methodist, United Reformed and Congregational Churches attended together with representatives from the Salvation Army and the Society of Friends. Tom Winning was joined by Bishop Mario Conti of Aberdeen, Bishop Colin MacPherson of Argyll and the Isles and Father Willy Slaven, of the Justice and Peace Commission, to make up the Roman Catholic contingent.

The eighty-nine year old Lord MacLeod of Fuinary set the ecumenical tone at this historic event, the first of its kind. A former Moderator of the Church of Scotland, a leading figure in the rebuilding of the Iona Abbey and the founder of its Community, he believed himself to be speaking prophetically when he told members of the assembled group:

We are commanded by Christ to have one church and a united church is coming. Not least the Roman Catholic Church's fashioning it. The seal seems to be set on the Roman Catholic Church leading us towards unity when we remember the Pope coming to Scotland two years ago. In Bellahouston Park he reminded us that we are only pilgrims on this earth and asked, 'Can we not make this pilgrimage together, hand-in-hand?'

On the first evening, Father Willy Slaven addressed the group on the need for the churches to become more committed to work for the disadvantaged at home and in the Third World. Canon Kenyon Wright, Secretary of the Scottish Churches' Council and Colonel Wesley Harris, Territorial Commander of the Salvation Army in Scotland led an Evening Service on the theme of Justice and Peace.

The second morning began with prayers led by Mrs Pat Welburn of the Iona Community and discussion followed a paper presented by another former Moderator, Professor John McIntyre, on attitudes to scripture and tradition in both the Roman Catholic and Presbyterian Churches. Then the group went on a symbolic pilgrimage to Columba's Bay where the saint landed in 561AD. The weather, as is often the case on Iona, was wet and windy and miserable. Tom Winning, now in his sixtieth year, was not sure, at first, if he should go on the long trek and he expressed his concerns *sotto voce* to a member of the Community. 'Don't worry,' this stalwart told him, 'I've a wee bottle of brandy which could come in handy.'

So Tom joined the pilgrimage to Columba's Bay but, as he anticipated, the wind, the rain and the fact that his waterproofs seemed to be preventing him from breathing properly, conspired to bring him to a halt. His ally from the Community came to his rescue, however; both of them slipped behind a large boulder and Tom took a good nip of the brandy. On the strength of it, he felt he could have walked on for forty days and forty nights! He was relieved to make it to the Bay, for the Reverend Ron Ferguson's Prayer Service and equally relieved that no one had seen him partake of the little fortification en route! This was one of many lighter moments during the two day session which concluded with a Service of Prayer for the Sick led by Tom Winning and former Moderator Dr William Johnston and an informal discussion on the topic: 'Where do we go from here?'

The get-together had concentrated more on what united the various denominations, though all present were well aware of the difficulties posed by questions of church unity: intercommunion, ministry, school policy, mixed marriages. These items would have to be high on future agendas, they could not be ducked.

As far as some Scots were concerned, though, the idea of unity
with the Catholic Church was anathema. Pastor Jack Glass had also
come to Iona – as a protester and not a pilgrim. He objected to Kirk
leaders talking to and praying with Roman Catholics and issued a
statement saying that the Pope's view of unity was 'the return of
Protestants to the Roman Catholic Church under his infallibility.'

The United Free Church also wanted no dialogue with Catholics.
In 1986, Pope John Paul called for another ecumenical gathering to
pray for peace. He met with church leaders in Assisi and, in solidarity
with this, Tom Winning initiated another meeting on Iona. There
was a good response from most of the other denominations, but the
United Free Church told Tom that it did not believe in saints or pil-
grimages and was not interested in any meetings designed to promote
unity.

Some years later, when the Perth Council of Churches invited the
archbishop to preach at St John's Kirk as the culmination to a week of
prayer for Christian unity, Pastor Glass and some hundred Protestant
demonstrators again voiced their disapproval. The Pastor threw thirty
pieces of silver through the doors of the Kirk, shouting that the council members were 'Judases'. He also smashed a clay bust of Pope John
XXIII – presumably because he had been known as 'the ecumenical
Pope' – on the pavement, in what he described as a symbolic protest in
the name of John Knox. In 1559, Knox had preached from the pulpit
of St John's, giving a sermon which was to start the Reformation in
motion. Tom Winning was the first member of the Catholic hierarchy
ever to have spoken from that same pulpit. The service was interrupted
three times by hecklers and he required police protection to shield
him from the jostling demonstrators as he made his way to a reception afterwards. Nevertheless, he was not unduly upset. The response
he had been given by the congregation at St John's was positive, and
later on that year, 1990, the Scottish Churches' Council was replaced
by a new body, Action of Churches Together in Scotland (ACTS). In
this the Catholic Church became a full participating member, rather
than having merely observer status, as on the council. The forming of
ACTS constituted a big change in the structure of institutionalised
ecumenism, as it approached unity from a different point of view.
The work done by the Scottish Churches' Council was the responsibility of those at the top of their own individual churches and never

got down to the ordinary people in the parishes. Taking the words of the Pope on his visit to Scotland to heart – '… not strangers but pilgrims going together …' – ACTS was to involve people from different Christian churches coming together, learning about each other and becoming involved in services of different kinds. Theological input would come from church leaders but it was to be largely 'grassroots' ecumenical activity and as such represented progress on the journey towards unity. All denominations were now facing the problem of declining membership and more and more church-goers were coming to the realisation that in the interests of the survival of Christianity in Scotland it would be necessary for the churches to move on from the conflicts of the past to full co-operation and commitment to the idea of communion with one another.

That there would be dissenting voices for a long time to come was something which Tom Winning acknowledged in his sermon at St John's Kirk: 'Nobody can force feed us unity. God alone knows how long it will take to chisel away the hardness of the human heart …'

There were significant changes in church personnel and a centralisation of administration and seminary training during the decade. Cardinal Gordon Gray, Archbishop of St Andrews and Edinburgh retired. His post as archbishop was given to Father Keith O'Brien, formerly the Rector of Blairs College, and Tom, now the senior member of the hierarchy, became President of the Scottish Bishops' Conference. In 1983, Bishop Joe Devine, one of Tom's two auxiliaries was appointed Bishop of Motherwell after Bishop Thomson's retiral and was replaced by Father John Mone. Donny Renfrew's health had deteriorated over the years: diabetes had resulted in kidney problems and the necessity for regular dialysis. He remained Tom's friend and 'sparring partner', never afraid to criticise him in private or offer advice. His ability to get around had lessened considerably but his sharp mind was put to good use in organising administrative affairs in the archdiocese. His job was made easier when the offices – previously located in Park Circus, Carlton Place and Newton Place – were centralised in a plush new glass building in Clyde Street, next door to St Andrew's Cathedral.

It had taken two years for the church to be given planning permission to erect the building on the site of what had once been a Cremola Custard Powder factory and then a printing works and studio. At the same time as the offices were constructed, the refurbishment of the cathedral, which Tom Winning had postponed more that ten years before, was carried out at a cost of over one million pounds. The priests' house attached to the cathedral was in such a dangerous condition that it had to be demolished. It was expensive to rebuild as it had to blend in with the A-listed St Andrew's. The offices themselves cost two and a half million pounds to build and the archbishop was criticised for what some considered to be profligacy.

A columnist in *The Glasgow Herald* dubbed the new buildings 'Marcinkus Mansions', a satiric reference to the Archbishop from Chicago, Paul Marcinkus, a friend of Tom Winning's during his student days in Rome and bodyguard to Pope John Paul. Some years previously, Marcinkus had hit the headlines in connection with his other job as Head of the Vatican Bank. Officially known as the Institute for the Works of Religion, the bank had been alleged to have had debts to the Banco Ambrosiano, which it did not wish to acknowledge and which apparently came to light when Robert Calvi, the Ambrosiano's President was found, hanged, under Blackfriars Bridge in London. The Vatican's finances had come under close scrutiny for some time after this, not least by Pope John Paul II, and while the Archdiocese of Glasgow, by 1988, was creaking under the weight of a four million pounds debt, this seemed small beer in comparison to the Holy See's 68 million dollar deficit which even Peter's pence, the annual offering which Catholics worldwide are asked to make to the papal coffers, could not make up.

But everything, as they say, is relative, and when an 'Open Day' was held to let the Glasgow clergy see the new offices, very few of them turned up. They were, apparently, concerned about costs. A debt of four million pounds seemed a financial crisis of mammoth proportions. What did the archbishop think he was doing, spending all that money on a big glass building?

However, the truth of the matter was that the new offices would make the church more efficient, practical and economical. The three costly Victorian buildings which had previously constituted the archdiocesan administration were sold off. Everything related to the management of the church was now under one roof: the Pastoral Centre, the Religious Education Centre, the Youth Council, the *Flourish* Office and so on. Overheads were reduced and, instead of being hidden away in various parts of the city, the 'engine room' of the church was now right in the centre of Glasgow, overlooking the River Clyde. It was a number of other factors which, over thirty years, had given rise to the archdiocese's financial situation.

Only about thirty per cent of the Catholic population was now attending Mass in the eighties, in comparison to seventy per cent in pre-Vatican II days. Moreover, attenders were not ensuring that the amount they put into Sunday church collections was commensurate with the increase in inflation. Sixty-four pence per person per week was the average contribution. For years the church had been helping poorer parishes with money from its central funds at an internal church rate of three per cent, but borrowing from banks at nearly four times that rate in order to do so. Maintenance and repair of church buildings constituted a regular financial burden and, in contrast to thirty years before, priests were being cared for in later life. In the past, they simply died in harness. Now there were forty ageing clergy to look after in retirement.

As well as collecting a levy from each parish (which could afford it) to pay for central services, the archdiocese also borrowed from parishes which operated at a surplus. In 1987, Tom Winning decided to increase the levy to help with expenditure and bank overdraft interest. There had been an overall increase of five and a half per cent in Sunday church offerings, thanks to an appeal the previous year. At the end of the decade he was appealing again for help to lessen debts, encouraging those parishioners who paid tax to sign Deeds of Covenant.

The closing and sale of Blairs College, the Junior Seminary in Aberdeen, which became a timeshare leisure complex, meant less money to be paid out by the archdiocese for its upkeep; but the fact that the ever-decreasing number of boys applying for the priesthood had resulted in the college's closure was indicative of another serious problem which the church in Scotland, and not just in Glasgow, had to face.

In 1985, a move was made towards unifying seminary education in Scotland when St Peter's College, serving Glasgow and Paisley, and St Andrew's College in Drygrange in the east of Scotland serving all other dioceses, were merged in the new Chesters College in Bearsden in Glasgow. When Tom ordained eight men in Glasgow four years later it was an occasion of great jubilation, but that fruitful year was followed by a barren year: in 1990, only one man was ordained to work in the Archdiocese in Glasgow. On the front page of the February edition of *Flourish,* the president of the city's Serra Club, an organisation seeking to promote vocations awareness, was highly critical of the apathy shown by priests and parishioners in respect of encouragement of young people to follow the religious life: 'The Pope has pointed out that the vitality of a parish could be gauged by the number of vocations it produces,' wrote Alex Duncan. 'If that is so, we must have a lot of dead parishes in Glasgow. What are our people thinking about? Unless we get our act together now, the 'Parish Closed' sign will be going up in many churches a lot sooner than we might care to admit …'

The idea of priestless parishes being a feature of the church of the future began to underline the importance of the lay person in the pastoral plan for the archdiocese, for those interested enough to 'read the signs of the times.' Perhaps members of parish, deanery and diocesan assemblies – the structures set in place by Tom Winning in the eighties – might find that a vital part of their agendas in the next millennium would be to consider how lay people should be trained and selected to take charge of parishes experiencing reduced sacramental provision.

Few Catholics have failed to see the irony of sermons exhorting young men to consider the priesthood as a vocation being preached to church congregations largely comprised of women. However the ordination of women would never be a pastoral option in the lifetime of Pope John Paul II. Nor would the celibacy rule be changed.

Tom Winning believed that the pessimism regarding falling numbers of new priests in the archdiocese should be weighed against an optimism based on the emergence of greater lay participation in church life.

His pastoral plan, with its emphasis on making lay people more actively involved in their local churches, could, in the future, be the means of keeping 'Parish Closed' signs at bay.

CHAPTER THIRTEEN

The Cardinal

In 1990, Archbishop Tom Winning became a 'senior citizen', but like his predecessor James Donald Scanlan, at the same age, he had no intention of retiring. The slim young man who had become bishop twenty years before was now stocky in build, his dark hair white. He was amused to read about himself in a book on churchmen in Britain, in which the writer had described him as looking and sounding like 'an artisan', obviously thinking it was inappropriate to say that an archbishop had the appearance and manner of a working man, a miner's son.

His family, Margaret his sister, her husband and their two children, had continued to be of great importance to him and he officiated at the weddings of his niece and nephew and christened their children. He was saddened by the deaths of friends from student days such as that of Hugh McEwan who had been ordained with him in 1948 and John McQuade with whom he had studied canon law and worked alongside in Motherwell.

With the retiral of Bishop Stephen McGill, John Mone became Bishop of Paisley. He was not replaced and Tom Winning and Donny Renfrew – whose health continued to limit the amount of work he could do – were assisted in matters such as the administration of confirmation, by the new vicar general, Father James Clancy. Such help was essential, because as President of the Bishops' Conference, Tom was often called abroad, particularly to Rome. In recent years, it had been part of Pope John Paul II's pastoral programme to gather bishops together from all different parts of the world to help him solve specific problems: thus there had been a Synod for the bishops of African countries, another for those from Holland. Tom represented the Scottish hierarchy at a meeting in Hungary of the Presidents of the Bishops' Conferences of Europe in 1990. There he met bishops from Central and Eastern Europe to talk about their common problems and this resulted in a European Synod in Rome the following year. In 1991 he also met with the Pope, the Eastern patriarchs – Raphael Bidawid of Baghdad, Michael Sabbah of Jerusalem and the bishops of those countries which had been involved in the Gulf War, to discuss the effects brought about by Iraq's invasion of Kuwait on the Christian communities in the Middle East. The church leaders talked about the war's impact on the links between Islam, Judaism and Christianity and considered how they could contribute to a lasting peace.

At home, the anti-war stance Tom Winning had taken during the Gulf crisis, although supported by some, was considered to be subversive by others. Thirteen and a half thousand Scots soldiers were among the British force of thirty-thousand involved in the war in the Gulf and whether it was a 'just' conflict or not was a subject which racked the consciences of many. Tom had been emphatically against the war from the start, believing that diplomacy rather than an escalation of military tension should be the priority. Given the destructive power of present day weapons, he feared an 'unspeakable holocaust' would result if it were not. Though he said that Saddam Hussein's behaviour in invading Kuwait could not be justified, nevertheless he felt that Britain should examine its reasons for involvement in the Gulf: was it for peace and justice or to protect its own oil supplies? For him, the war was the 'poisoned fruit' of Western nations' arms trade with Third World Countries. The Moderator, the Primus of the Scottish Episcopal Church and representatives of the Congregational Methodist, United Free Church and the Society of Friends joined him in writing a letter to the Foreign Secretary, Douglas Hurd, expressing the view that 'war is no foundation for peace', but not all church leaders felt the same and the fact that Cardinal Hume of Westminster did not take the same line as Glasgow's archbishop caused certain sections of the media to try to encourage 'in-fighting' between them. Hume expressed the view that ultimately only politicians could decide when options short of force had been proved to fail and war became inevitable. He believed that the war was a 'tragic necessity' and, like the Archbishop of Canterbury, supported the British conservative government's involvement in the Gulf.

Those Scottish churchmen who adopted an anti-war stance were criticised for undermining the morale of Scottish troops and the Convener of the General Assembly's Committee on Chaplains to

Her Majesty's Forces, the Reverend Alistair Symington, was reported in *The Glasgow Herald* of 21 January 1991 as stating that the position taken by the national churches ignored the realities of men and women in need, especially those in the front-line of the hostilities. Tom Winning was undeterred by those who believed he was being disloyal to Britain and should keep his mouth shut about political matters. He continued to say that war should never be an option for settling disputes among nations. All parish priests in the Archdiocese of Glasgow received a letter from him telling them to seek out families, relatives and friends of people involved in the conflict, in order to offer them support. Masses for peace were held throughout the city and members of the Moslem community joined Catholics in St Andrew's Cathedral to pray for an end to hostilities.

The Gulf War Memorial Service, which was held after the conflict was over, caused nearly as much controversy as whether or not the war had been 'just'. The government had decided that the Service was to take place in Glasgow Cathedral, in acknowledgement of the considerable contribution made by Scottish soldiers to the allied effort. Dr William Morris, the minister of the cathedral, was asked to organise the event, a weighty task given that it would be a state occasion. Scotish church leaders were invited to take part in the Service but, to emphasise its national breadth, Dr Morris asked the Anglican Archbishop of York, Dr John Habgood, to be the preacher. Glaswegian Moslem and Jewish children, as well as Christian, were also asked to read prayers in the cathedral.

Some newspapers reported that leading figures in the Church of Scotland were unhappy about the lack of consultation and ecumenical planning for the service, while the Episcopalian Bishop of Edinburgh, the Right Reverend Richard Holloway, felt that if there was to be a service, then a Scots clergyman should have been asked to preach. His main point, though, was that there should be no service at all, while people in the conflict area were still suffering. There was a general concern lest the service, to be attended by the Queen and the Prime Minister, Mr John Major, and relatives of those who had been killed in the war, should become triumphalist in tone.

Tom Winning expressed no opinion in public regarding the service to be held on 4 May. However, he did have a problem with the wording of a prayer which had been written for him to say in the

cathedral, the draft copy of which he received on 22 April. He felt
that he could not in conscience read the words: 'Turn the hearts of all
who have been our enemies to the truth, as you have revealed it in
Jesus, that they may know and do your will', which had been written
for him. He did not want to recite a prayer implying that the Iraqis
should be converted to Christianity, preferring to pray for reconciliation. A request for these words to be changed and a note of other
minor adjustments were delivered by hand to Dr Morris at the cathedral on 24 April but unfortunately the Order of Service had already
been printed and bound the previous day. A compromise was
reached and Tom Winning's own version of the prayer was included
in the Order of Service book on a separate sheet.

His communications with Dr Morris had been private but some
how the media got hold of the story. 'I cannot say Gulf Service
Prayers: Archbishop's Thanksgiving Day Bombshell.' was how the
Edinburgh Evening News described it. 'Winning in Gulf Service War
of Words,' ran *The Glasgow Herald* headline. But the Archbishop
had never, at any time, refused to say prayers, buty merely asked for
alterations, nor had he engaged in any confrontations over the matter.
In the event his own prayer for all the victims of the 'bitter harvest of
injury and death, illness and pain, homelessness and hunger' was his
contribution to ensuring that the Service was reconciliatory and not
triumphalist.

Tom Winning's position on the war issue was not popular with
many people, but succeeded in enhancing the Catholic Church's
image in the eyes of Glasgow's Moslem community: the Young
Moslem Movement invited him to the Central Mosque to discuss
the Middle East situation with them.

Tom Winning's compelling need to speak out against what he believed to be evils in society caused controversy in the media again, in
the summer of 1991, when he took the Labour Party to task concerning its policy on abortion. With the country in the midst of pre-elec-
tion fever, the editorial of the July issue of *Flourish* delivered what
Father Tom Connelly, the church's media spokesman, described as 'a
warning shot across Labour's bows'. For more than seventy years, the
majority of Catholics had traditionally voted Labour because it was
perceived to be committed to social justice and appealed to the working class of which the largely Irish immigrant Catholic population

formed a part. 'But has Labour taken the much publicised Catholic vote for granted for too long?' asked the archbishop, through the columns of his newspaper. '… Have Catholics taken the Labour Party for granted and perhaps too uncritically, to the point of short-sightedness?'

He went on to question whether the Labour Party any more than any other was in the best position to reflect Catholic voters' Christian priorities, noting that Labour was the only major political party committed to extending abortion provision. He named and thanked those Scottish MPs from within and near the archdiocese who had taken a pro-life stand, but stated that their position should not mask the 'wave of persecution' which was emerging against those in the party who were disregarding official pro-abortion policy. 'The mother's womb had ceased to be a sanctuary and has become a medical killing ground,' he said, asking if the fact that same Labour MPs had advocated the publication of a blacklist of doctors who refused to take part in abortions was 'a taste of things to come'. 'The pro-life credentials of individual candidates and of political parties should, I believe, play a crucial role in deciding who we vote for,' was his conclusion, 'we should think long and hard before we vote for someone who is prepared to permit the killing of unborn babies.'

The response from the Labour Party to Tom Winning's comments was a resounding silence. Shadow Secretary Donald Dewar and Councillor Charles Gray, the leader of Strathclyde's Labour administration, both declined to comment. *The Daily Record,* the most popular tabloid newspaper in the country, decided to respond on their behalf, stating in their 'View' of 6 July that: 'the Labour Party had not responded to the archbishop's attack presumably on the basis of least said, soonest mended. But the *Record* cannot remain silent. While respecting the archbishop's views and his right to express them, we have to remind him of the dangers of people voting on religious lines instead of their social and political beliefs.'

Brian Meek, a conservative, wrote in *The Glasgow Herald* on 8 July, 'I thought that Archbishop Winning was wrong about the Gulf War and I said so. He is wrong again.' He continued: 'The fact that the Labour Party cannot say that, out of fear of tangling with the church, hardly underlines their credibility as an alternative government …' 'All the sensible Roman Catholics, the ones who just somehow manage to have only a couple of kids, will pay not the slightest attention to the archbishop ...'

Tom Winning was not surprised at the vilification his article had aroused but he was angry that neither these newspapers nor any others had attempted to address the subject of abortion nor consider Labour's policies regarding it. Instead they had condemned him for having the audacity to speak out about it to his community while, at the same time, felt it was their place to advise people on how much or little notice they should take of his opinion. 'These newspapers have no right, no duty, no mandate whatsoever to advise their Catholic readers on moral, ethical or theological matters,' he replied, through the columns of the *Scottish Catholic Observer*, 'Why did none of them address the subject of abortion? Why are they so scared?'

Labour's official silence was broken by the MP for Glasgow Provan, Jimmy Wray. *The Sunday Times* of 14 July reported him as: 'calling upon Archbishop Winning to button his lip' and inviting him to get around the table with party officials to discuss abortion, rather than launching attacks through the media. Wray's remark that Winning was 'getting a lot of people's backs up' encapsulated what he very often did when speaking from his position as Archbishop of Glasgow. No one was ever left in any doubt regarding his opinion which, on ethical matters, was uncompromising. He never flagged in his efforts to encourage Catholics to stand up, be counted and get involved, if they wished to change society. He took it upon himself to be a burr in the conscience of his community. It did not make him popular.

1992 began with both joy and sorrow. On 9 January, the church celebrated its five hundredth anniversary, recalling the year, 1492, when Pope Innocent VIII made Glasgow an archdiocese. For many Catholics, it was astonishing to think that their church was so well established as far back as the time when Christopher Columbus was 'discovering' America and that the city's first archbishop, Robert Blacader, provided Christian aid to the Glasgow community in the form of a hospital for lepers.

Of course, for about half of those five hundred years the archdiocese existed in name only, with Catholicism being virtually wiped out of the area as a result of the Reformation. St Andrew's Cathedral, where the celebration Mass took place in 1992, was well able to hold

the entire Catholic population of Glasgow and surrounding area
when it was first established in 1816. The church's survival and
growth was a cause for thanksgiving and celebration and the quincentenary was used as an opportunity not just to reflect on past history
but to look to the future.

The archbishop launched two initiatives: a trust, to exist until the
end of the century, for pastoral and social care, the aim being to raise
one million pounds a year, a total of eight million in all, available to
people in the Glasgow community on the basis of need and regard-
less of religious affiliation. A team was set up, chaired by Glasgow
businessman, Brian Dempsey, to organise innovative methods of
fund raising. On behalf of the archdiocese, Tom Winning also donated
a Chair to the University of Glasgow for the Study of the Child.

Writing about these ventures in *Flourish,* he stated:

'The church has been – is – and will continue to be good news for
Glasgow. The quincentenary celebrations will be an opportunity
for the church in Glasgow to express solidarity with all people,
especially those in need.

The presence of so many representatives from the state, the other
churches and faith communities at our Thanksgiving Mass is a
measure of the importance of the Catholic community in
Scotland. My hope for this year is that we will become an even
more significant force for good in our society …'

Liturgical events were arranged throughout the city in order that
celebrations could continue for the course of the year. By February,
however, the church was in mourning when Charles 'Donny'
Renfrew died, the archdiocese's auxiliary bishop and the man whom
Tom Winning regarded as his best friend.

He had often thought of how he would cope with Donny's passing. Although Tom was older than his friend, he knew that with all
Donny's health problems, he was unlikely to live into old age. Privately,
he felt that if the bishop had lived in a previous time in the church's
history, he would have been considered a saint. The equanimity and
good humour with which he endured his many illnesses, his obvious
and yet never off-putting holiness, made him a favourite with the
Glasgow people. The number which turned out to his funeral Mass was
testimony to that.

Tom found it difficult to sleep during the nights following Donny's death and prior to his Requiem. His mind was full of memories, vivid pictures of the past. What could he say about his assistant, the one person to whom he could really unburden his heart? What kind of panegyric would be fitting?

It was when lying in bed and listening to the birds' exuberant dawn chorus that he finally got his inspiration. What made Charles Renfrew 'sing'?

He thought of his friend's profound love of the church, his passion for reading, writing and a good argument. He remembered the fun they had had in Rome and the panache with which Donny directed the Gilbert and Sullivan operettas.

Then there was his sense of humour, his way with people, his love of football and deep affection for Glasgow. Latterly, of course, with failing sight and failing health, it was prayer and the spiritual life which made Donny 'sing' and gave enrichment and clear purpose to his existence.

The more jubilantly the birds whistled outside Tom's window, the more uplifted his spirits became. Thus the homily which he wrote later and delivered at Donny's funeral emphasised pride in and thanksgiving for the 'song' which was his friend's life rather than the sorrow and sense of loss brought about by his death. He caused the huge congregation gathered at St Peter's Church in Partick to laugh heartily by mimicking what Donny would have said concerning his own panegyric: 'Get someone else to deliver it, Tom, you'll only make a hash of it!'

In effect, his farewell to Bishop Renfrew was truly fitting, capturing as it did, the essence of a genuinely good man. Perhaps Donny had sent the birds to sing outside Tom's room to make sure his exit would be on an upbeat note!

The quincentenary celebrations continued as planned. The Senate of Strathclyde University thought it an appropriate time to honour Tom for his work in Glasgow. On 10 April he was invited to join, among other distinguished graduands, Lord Charles Forte of Ripley, in the Barony Graduation Hall, where he became the recipient of yet another honorary degree. At the ceremony, his 'compassion for the disadvantaged' was acknowledged and he was described as having 'considerably enriched the spiritual and social life of the community'.

Later in the year, another celebration was held, this time in Glasgow's Kelvin Hall, where ten thousand people assembled to partake in a Mass of thanksgiving. Tom was disappointed that Gordon Gray had been unable to join in any of the celebrations. The cardinal had sent a warm message of congratulations to his 'sister' metropolitan See and regretted that he could not come to Glasgow because of 'age and infirmity'.

Tom must have thought that the increasing years had caught up with him too, when in August of 1992, on his return from a demanding trip visiting Glasgow missionaries in Kenya, he was rushed to Ruchill hospital with a debilitating mystery illness. An exhaustive series of tests confirmed that he was not suffering from any tropical disease but had a serious form of influenza. The *Evening Times* of 25 August described him as 'the fifty year old' in their front page article headed 'Winning Malaria Scare' but Tom was now sixty-seven. Despite his youthful appearance, he no longer had the energy of former years and the African trip took a lot out of him. He made a complete recovery, but was at last beginning to learn the importance of pacing himself.

Cardinal Gray, Tom's senior by sixteen years, did not regain his health and the church in Scotland was saddened when, in 1993, the old prelate died. He had been the first resident Scot in four hundred years to be elected to the College of Cardinals and had led the Scottish hierarchy during Vatican II.

Not surprisingly, Gordon Gray's death gave rise to much rumour both in the press and in the church in general. Everyone began to speculate as to who would be the next cardinal. Some said surely it would be Archbishop Winning as he was the senior churchman and President of the Bishops' Conference. Others said no, since Archbishop Keith O'Brien had succeeded Cardinal Gray in St Andrews and Edinburgh, he must be the next cardinal. After all, Edinburgh was the capital city. So the gossip continued.

A month after Cardinal Gray's death, the Vatican's representative in Britain, the Apostolic Pro Nuncio, Archbishop Luigi Barbarito, was on a visit to the diocese of Galloway. There he attempted to put an end to the rumours. 'Any such appointment would be a personal decision of the Pope,' Barbarito said in an interview for the Catholic press. 'It is likely to be several years before there is an intake to the

College of Cardinals and even then there is no certainty of a Scottish appointment.'

Tom himself hoped that the rumours would abate. The talk of 'red hats' was putting him under a degree of psychological pressure he could well have done without.

The gossip among the clergy and those lay people who liked to think that they were 'in the know' began to change. Some said their archbishop would retire at seventy and that he'd 'missed the boat' as far as being made a cardinal was concerned. When the Belgian archbishop, Cardinal Suenens retired, his successor in Brussels was named cardinal too, and within a short time of his appointment. Yet Cardinal Gray had been retired for eight years before his death and still the Vatican had made no moves to create another cardinal in Scotland.

Some newspaper articles focused on the archdiocesan debt which had, at one period, soared to nine million pounds. The implication was that Tom had not been 'looking after the shop' and the stories that some archdiocesan employees had reputedly mismanaged funds in the church's Social Services Department served to reinforce this notion. Tom Winning was too busy trying to get his church's bank balance 'into the black' to be worried about 'going into the red' himself! The fact that Tom had inherited a great deal of debt which, due to inflation, had soared, and that his five year financial plan to deal with it by means of second collections in parishes and the sale of property was bringing in just under a million pounds a year, was not acknowledged at this time. It was just as the gossip seemed to be dying down and interested parties beginning to think that any further speculation was futile, when things started to happen.

Tom had returned from a pilgrimage to the Holy Land on Sunday 22 October 1994, and was settling back into his normal routine. On the evening of the Thursday following his return, he took a break from working in his study at home to make himself a cup of tea. The telephone rang and he answered it.

'Could I speak to the Archbishop of Glasgow?' said the heavily accented Italian voice on the line. 'Oh, I recognise who this is,' said Tom. 'It's Archbishop Barbarito.' 'Yes, are you alone?' It was like Archbishop Enrici's call of twenty-three years before. 'Yes, I am alone,' Tom replied. 'I had to be very formal at the beginning,' said

Barbarito. 'I have to tell you that the Holy Father wishes to make you a cardinal.' 'My God,' said Tom, 'give me a moment to get my breath back!' 'There's to be thirty new cardinals,' Barbarito continued. 'You have to keep this secret until 11.00 a.m. Sunday morning and you'll receive written confirmation shortly.'

Tom had the presence of mind to ask if he could lift the embargo to tell Father Tom Connelly, the church's media representative and Father Peter Smith, the archdiocesan chancellor, in order that the necessary arrangements might be made. Barbarito understood that this was practical and agreed.

It was indeed very much like the situation of 1971 when, having been told to keep the news that he was to be made auxiliary bishop a secret from members of his family, Tom had to find a way of gathering them all together to break the news as soon as the time came for it to be officially announced. Once again, it was Hallowe'en and he told his relatives to come for lunch with strict instructions that they had to be at his home in Newlands by 10.30 a.m. on Sunday 30 October. Everyone wondered what was afoot.

Cardinal-elect or no, the mischievous devil in Tom Winning inevitably came to the surface. Father Noel Barry, the editor of *Flourish*, together with Fathers Connelly and Smith, were also invited to the lunch party. Father Barry was bursting with curiosity and was continually enquiring as to what it was all about, despite the others' explanations that it was totally confidential. When he arrived at 10.15 a.m. he asked what was happening. With a totally straight face his archbishop took him into the sitting room and said, 'I'm resigning,' turned on his heel and walked out, but not before catching sight of Father Barry's crestfallen expression as he moved rapidly over to the window and lit a cigarette. It was another three quarters of an hour before the unfortunate Barry was put out of his misery when he and Tom's relations were told that they now had a cardinal in their midst. All were jubilant.

Word of the announcement spread rapidly and congregations burst into applause as their priests told them the news during Sunday Mass. Messages of congratulations began to pour in from all over the city, the country and beyond. The Lord Provost of Glasgow, James Shields, stated that it was 'wonderful news for Tom Winning and for Glasgow' and would 'keep the city and Scotland to the fore'. Ian

Lang, the Secretary of State for Scotland, pronounced it: 'a great honour for the archbishop, the Scottish Catholic community and for Scotland in general' whilst the reactions of other religious leaders were equally positive. The Moderator, James Simpson, spoke of his delight at the appointment. Cardinal Cahal Daly, Archbishop of Armagh, expressed his joy that the 'very good friend to Ireland' had been elevated to the College of Cardinals, saying: 'He has been deeply committed to the process of reconciliation between the two great religious traditions once so deeply divided in his country as they have been in the northern part of our own land.'

The following morning the national newspapers carried the story and attempted to analyse the implications of the Archbishop of Glasgow's promotion. 'Scotland's status reinforced within the Catholic Church' ran the headline in *The Glasgow Herald*'s leader article, which went on to note that Glasgow now had its first cardinal in the city's history and the country its third since the Reformation.

Most papers featured the usual pen portrait, describing Tom as 'conservative on theological matters but outspoken on social and political issues' and explaining that he would now be eligible to vote for a new Pope at the next secret conclave in the Vatican. Theoretically, said religious commentators, Tom Winning could be made Pope himself. Citing his age as a reason, they considered this to be an unlikely development, although they did acknowledge that he would now have a more influential role in the formulation of church policy.

Cardinals were to be appointed from countries worldwide, a clear indication, it was thought, of John Paul II's continued desire to internationalise the Sacred College. As a result, this would increase the chances of his successor being a non-Italian. It was thought significant that many of the new cardinals came from places where the church had or continued to suffer hardship: the former Eastern bloc countries, for example. The Archbishop of Prague, Miloslav Vlk, had been forced to work as a window cleaner during the Czech communist regime, while carrying out his priestly ministry in secret. One of the oldest of the new cardinals, Father Mikel Koliqi, aged ninety-two, had spent many years in prison during the long period of communist dictatorship in Albania. The Archbishop of war-torn Sarajevo in Bosnia was to be given a red hat and church leaders of other communities under duress, the Patriarch of the Maronite Christians in the Lebanon, the Archbishops of Hanoi, Chile, Guadalajara and Havana were also to be honoured. Europe was well represented with French, Spanish, Belgian, Swiss and Germans being appointed. The new Italian cardinals were already high profile figures in the curia. Others came from as far afield as Tokyo, Indonesia, Kampala and Peru. The United States was to receive two red hats, going to the Archbishops of Baltimore and Detroit.

Such men would guarantee that the traditionalist and theologically conservative approach of John Paul II would be maintained, observed reporters, going so far as to describe Tom Winning as 'moderate' in comparison to some.

The date of the installation ceremony was set for 26 November and some fifteen hundred Scots made preparations to fly to Rome to support their new cardinal. Tom himself had to go a week in advance, to be kitted out in the new red garb that would now replace the archbishop's purple. Typical of the canny Scot, he felt irritated that he had recently spent £450 on a purple cassock for which he would now no longer have any use and could not help reflecting in amazement that the same outfit, of the same material, cost only £25 back in 1971!

He proved to all who followed him to Rome that he was still one of 'their ain folk'. There were few who could not have been impressed by the fact that he was there, at Rome airport, to greet the Scots arrivals and have a personal word with each one of them, and moreover, on the eve of his initiation into the College of Cardinals. This warm-hearted and courteous act set the tone for the five days' proceedings which were, by turns, solemn and dignified, festive, family-like and heartily Scottish. The presence of an accomplished young bagpipe player in the company ensured that the citizens of Rome were left in no doubt that the Scots had come to town.

The first of the ceremonies was the Consistory, when the cardinals were given their 'red hats' by the Holy Father, in the Vatican's huge Audience Hall. Twenty-nine of the thirty new cardinals were called upon to kneel before the Pope (the thirtieth, the well-known French theologian Yves Congar, was too ill to attend) as he pronounced in Latin:

> To the glory of God almighty and for the good of the Apostolic
> See, receive the red biretta as a sign of the dignity of a cardinal, as

a reminder that you must be ready to act with renewed vigour, up to the point of shedding your own blood, for the growth of the Christian faith, for peace and tranquillity of the people of God and the spread of the Holy Roman Catholic Church.

Tom Winning was fourth in line to be received by the Pope. When his name was called, in the church's ancient language, 'Thomam Iosephum Winning, Archiepiscopum Glasguensem,' the Scots present broke into rapturous applause. Television crews from around the world filmed the event from the cramped camera gallery situated high in the immense chamber named after Pope Paul VI. The priest from Craigneuk who had once firmly believed he would never be considered even for a post of parish priest was now a 'prince of the church'. His thoughts were with his mother and father who had been with him in Rome at his ordination in 1948. This time he was supported by his sister, her extended family and the fifteen hundred ecstatic Scots who assembled in the Piazza to greet him after the ceremony. Many were bedecked in tartan and some were waving a huge green banner on which was written the slogan: 'Cardinal Winning's Miles Better!' The skirl of the pipes – not a sound often heard in the precincts of St Peter's – provided a stirring accompaniment to the impromptu party.

The following day, the new cardinals joined Pope John Paul for Mass in the Basilica, during which they received gold rings, as symbols of their office. On Monday, a special audience was held for all the English-speaking visitors who had accompanied Cardinal Winning and Cardinals Keeler of Baltimore and Maida of Detroit to Rome. At this ceremony, the Pope addressed the cardinals and met their families. Once more, the atmosphere was distinctly Scottish. John Paul clearly loved the bagpipe playing; even the Swiss Guards, noted for their sang-froid in every circumstance, seemed almost impressed by the spectacle.

Tom was the first of the three cardinals to be addressed by the Pope:

Cardinal Winning, as priest and bishop you have always been what is called 'a man of the people' with a great personal sensitivity for the welfare of the less fortunate. In this, you show what it means to be a shepherd according to the mind and heart of Christ, who came to serve and not to be served. I know that the good

Catholic people of Glasgow will continue to support you and help you make the *Specialis filia romanae ecclesiae* (special Daughter of the Roman Church) an ever dearer witness to God's faithfulness and love. May Saint Andrew and Saint Margaret, Scotland's patrons, and Saint Mungo, special patron of Glasgow, intercede for all the bishops, priests and laity of your beloved land.

There were few Scottish hearts which did not swell with pride at that moment.

After the new cardinals introduced their families and close friends to the Pope, the audience ended to the tune of 'Flower of Scotland'. John Paul beamed, 'the tartan contingent' left the hall in great good humour and American reporters were heard to ask: 'Just who is this Cardinal Winning?'

Situated near the Trevi Fountain in Rome is the Basilica of Saint Andrea delle Fratte. It was here that the last of the ceremonies took place on the feast of Saint Andrew. By tradition, each cardinal is allocated a church as his 'titular' parish. Tom was granted Saint Andrea's, reputed to be the burial place of Bishop Turnbull, the founder of Glasgow University. The church's link with Scotland dated back to 1450, when it was used exclusively for large numbers of Scots visiting Rome in the Holy Year. Now, over five hundred years later, Scots crowded into the church again, to witness their new cardinal become its 'protector', as the Papal Bull of Appointment was read aloud during the Mass. Twenty-three years before, to the day, Tom had been made auxiliary bishop in St Andrew's Cathedral in Glasgow. Thus the ceremony in Saint Andrea's seemed an appropriate conclusion to the events of the previous four days.

It was the Right Reverend Professor Robert Davidson, former Moderator and Convenor of the ecumenical group ACTS, who, at the end of the Mass, was called upon to sum up the feelings of those from other churches and the Moslem and Jewish faiths, invited to join the celebrations in Rome. In so doing, he highlighted one of the areas of church life to which Tom Winning's contribution had been significant:

It was ... for all of us a warm and deeply moving occasion. When the history of the church in the second half of this century is written, it may well be called the age in which doors that had for too long been closed began to be opened. Our presence here is but the latest of many occasions on which Cardinal Winning has opened doors through which some of us have gladly walked ...'

Thus 1994 ended positively for the Catholic Church not just in Glasgow but in Scotland. Despite colossal rain and flooding, nine thousand parishioners from all over the country gathered at the Scottish Exhibition Centre on 11 December to express solidarity with their new cardinal. 'Outside it is windy, stormy and raining,' said Archbishop Luigi Barbarito, who was present, 'but here there is warmth and I feel a sense of spring which is the spring for the Catholic Church in Scotland.'

Coming from Italy it was not surprising that Barbarito had been rather sanguine in his choice of metaphor. Indeed it was a tremendous boost for Catholics to have their own cardinal once more, with all the prestige that the office carries with it.

Barbarito was not to know that many a snell wind blows in a Scottish spring: Catholics had only a relatively short time in which to bask in the reflected glory of Tom Winning's new position before their attention was suddenly and dramatically diverted. Alas for those who court hubris even just a little because humiliation seems sure to follow.

The new cardinal had experienced the greatest honour his church could bestow upon him. He was still to face the very worst event in his ecclesiastical career. This occurred some eighteen months after he took up his new office, when a member of his own hierarchy became involved in a lurid sex scandal which set the church in turmoil.

CHAPTER FOURTEEN

Crisis? What Crisis?

Roderick Wright, Bishop of Argyll and the Isles, had been among the crowds in St Peter's square cheering on Cardinal Winning in November 1994.

No one would have believed that sometime previously, Bishop Wright had been interviewed by Tom Winning and Archbishop Keith O'Brien of St Andrews and Edinburgh, to respond to allegations that he had been engaging in illicit relationships with female members of his diocese.

Bishop Wright vehemently denied the allegations, saying that they were nothing more than scurrilous rumours. Archbishop Winning, as he then was, accepted Wright's 'cast-iron' guarantees. If he had been less trusting or, as some saw it, less naïve, the furore of September 1996, might have been avoided and Wright given the counselling it became obvious he so badly needed. The fact that Tom Winning did not carry out sufficiently thorough investigations of his own in Argyll diocese proved to be a serious misjudgement.

The controversy started on Sunday 8 September, when Bishop Joe Devine received a telephone call from the Argyll diocese telling him that Bishop Wright would not be able to preach at the annual pilgrimage Mass in Carfin, Lanarkshire, as he appeared to have gone missing. By the following weekend, national news bulletins were announcing that the bishop had gone AWOL, and that church officials were concerned that he should inform them of his whereabouts and let them know if he was well. Rumours were rife: some said he had been suffering from stress, others that he had gone off with a female parishioner with whom he was known to be very friendly and who had also been reported missing. Feelings in the church were compassionate: the bishop was well-liked, his health and safety were the main concern.

By the following weekend the situation was becoming clearer: Bishop Wright had indeed left his diocese with a divorcee and mother of three but no one knew where he had gone. The *Sunday Mail* tabloid newspaper had the story splashed across its front page with a picture of the bishop wearing his mitre. There was also a photograph of a middle-aged woman, scantily clad. The *Mail* described the developments as 'the biggest love scandal ever to hit Scotland'.

The drama continued as the weekend drew to a close, when Bishop Wright met with Cardinal Winning and Archbishop O'Brien at the cardinal's home in Newlands. In a highly emotional state he offered his resignation to the cardinal. He wanted to quit because not only had he been having a liaison with a female parishioner, he also had a fifteen-year-old son from a previous relationship. Archbishops Winning and O'Brien were aghast at this revelation but still entreated the bishop not to do anything rash while in his present state of mind. The bishop disappeared in haste, however, leaving Tom Winning in the unenviable position of having to deal with this information in the best way possible for all concerned, given that he felt duty bound to respect the privacy of the bishop's son and the boy's mother.

Cardinal Winning did not reveal this aspect of the bishop's background, which appeared to become increasingly sensational by the hour, when he met with the media at a press conference in the archdiocesan offices the following day. To say the cardinal was ill at ease was an understatement. Ashen-faced, shaken, his eyes red-rimmed, he read a resignation statement on behalf of Roddy Wright which stated that the bishop felt physically and spiritually incapable of sustaining his responsibilities and asking for prayers and forgiveness. The door would always be open to him, the cardinal said, to take up priestly duties in some form, somewhere, if he chose to return. The church was a church for sinners and bishops would be forgiven too.

It was a major embarrassment for the hierarchy and a severe blow to the Catholic population, particularly those in Argyll whose priests had met with the cardinal that morning at Fort Augustus Abbey. It did not end there, however, for before the end of the week, the mother of Bishop Wright's son revealed her situation and Wright's deceit to the BBC. Bishop Wright, who had gone off to the Lake District with his current companion, finally sold his story to *The News of the World*.

Catholics were left reeling by these bizarre events and for the cardinal it was ignominious. He was accused of covering up the full extent of the errant bishop's misdemeanours and thus prolonging the situation as the details were only gradually revealed. He defended his decision to keep the information private, stating that he would have been castigated even more if he had usurped what was the right of the boy's mother to reveal, and her right alone. It was, on his own admission, the worst experience in Tom Winning's career in twenty-five years as a senior churchman. He felt he had been totally duped by Wright who, one week appeared to be full of remorse and the following week, rather than returning to explain his behaviour to his own people in Argyll, chose to speak to newspaper reporters instead.

'I want to apologise on behalf of the church to Catholics everywhere,' said Bishop Mario Conti of Aberdeen as the scandal reached its height. Tom Winning was finding it difficult to step over his door in the face of the inquisitorial glare of the media and relied upon his senior colleagues to respond to journalists. The informed and the uninformed debated the rule of priestly celibacy on TV and radio chat shows and the transgressions of other clergy were revealed in minute detail in the tabloid press. Some priests in Scotland found it was safer not to wear clerical dress in the street and went about their duties in mufti, such was the degree of harassment that started to develop. Those who made a living from comedy had enough material to last them for months and indeed the farcical elements of the situation could not be denied. The beleaguered Father Tom Connelly, the church's media spokesman, who looked increasingly fraught with every TV interview he gave, on one occasion spoke of the abuse and smutty jokes to which priests were being subjected as they 'tried to carry on their legitimate affairs'.

The quest by some newspapers for more and more sordid details continued to escalate, with friends and relatives of those involved in the scandal, as well as priests, being besieged and intimidated in their own homes in the early morning and late at night. Cardinal Winning complained that some elements of the tabloid press were like the gestapo in Britain in the 1990s. His own housekeeper was seriously frightened when a reporter pressed the doorbell of his house and would not stop until the police were called. On 26 September the cardinal decided that enough was enough and issued an open letter to newspaper editors in which he stated that the church would no longer participate in satisfying the speculative demands of the media. 'Celibacy is not the issue, nor is it the crisis the media would have us

believe,' he wrote. 'One man's highly publicised indiscretions which
have become a crisis for the media, do not constitute a crisis for the
church.' So the door of the church would always be open to the
erring Roddy Wright, but was firmly closed on the faces of the voracious
elements of the press.

The heat was largely taken out of the situation as a result of
Cardinal Winning's letter, but the 'Crisis – what crisis?' line which he
adopted was rather difficult for a number of Catholics to accept, as
they had always believed their bishops were above reproach. The
moral authority of the clergy had received a severe testing and Tom
Winning came in for the most severe criticism. Why had he not been
more rigorous in investigating the allegations against Roddy Wright
in Argyll itself? How had Wright reached such a high position in the
church in the first place? As head of the Bishops' Conference, it was
surely up to Winning to check on the conduct of the hierarchy.

Those who were pro-celibacy said that allowing priests to marry
would not prevent such things happening – ordinary married men
had affairs too. The Roddy Wright debacle served to strengthen the
argument for having women priests, some thought. Perhaps women
were constitutionally more able to deal with the celibate life, if that
was what was required in the priestly ministry.

No-one seriously expected Tom Winning to change his views in a
'knee-jerk' reaction to the scandal, or an announcement to be issued
from Rome regarding any reversal to the age-old church tradition of
an all male, celibate clergy. Bloodied but unbowed, Cardinal Winning
was determined that the church would not be side-tracked from its
central beliefs and those who had been hurt most by the behaviour of
Roddy Wright should be helped to heal. He made regular visits to
Argyll and the Isles and Archbishop Keith O'Brien was given special
responsibility for it. Three years elapsed before the diocese had a replacement bishop. Time enough to let the dust settle, perhaps?
Eventually, Keith O'Brien's vicar general, Monsignor Ian Murray,
was appointed in Wright's place. It would be a hard act to follow.

Father Noel Barry, the well-respected editor of the Glasgow archdiocesan newspaper, *Flourish,* and one of Cardinal Winning's closest
aides, also fell foul of the media. He took out a case against *The Sun*
newspaper for printing an article in 1996 which, he believed, implied
a sexual relationship between himself and a female friend and dam-

aged their reputation. The jury at the Court of Session in Edinburgh found in favour of Father Barry and his friend but the effect of the surrounding publicity made it seem, to outside observers at least, rather a pyrrhic victory. *The Sun* had contacted another woman, whom Father Barry had met during the eighties. It was made public during the court proceedings that he had been in love with this person, a former nun, but her version of their relationship, given on the 17 December 1998, contrasted with Father Barry's. He had kept his vow of celibacy, Father Barry had said. But the woman he had loved stated that this was just not true and proceeded to present her own account of their liaison, giving highly personal details to the court.

Cardinal Winning had received a summons to appear in the witness box on the following day, 18 December, but at noon was told that he would not be required after all. It was the fiftieth anniversary of his ordination to the priesthood but the cardinal did not feel like celebrating.

Reports relating to what had been said in court the previous day featured in the Scottish papers. There were some melodramatic headlines: one two-page spread was prefaced by the words: 'Sins of the flesh'. The cardinal was presented as having been harsh and unhelpful to the lady when she had visited him to 'reveal' her relationship with Father Barry. Whatever the truth of the situation, to many Catholics it looked like one sorry mess and left them thinking, 'What next?'

When Cardinal Winning did mark his fiftieth anniversary of ordination to the priesthood, with a Mass in the City Halls in January 1999, he was surrounded by fifteen hundred lay people, more than one hundred priests, twenty-one bishops, two cardinals and the Papal Nuncio, together with VIPs from various sectors of Scottish society. But on the TV news bulletins that Sunday evening, it was the presence of Father Barry which was highlighted and he was shown seated alongside the other clergy during the Mass.

During his sermon, the cardinal thanked a number of people, including the representatives from the media who were present and caused considerable laughter by his ironic reference to the 'no end of bother' which they took in order to report on the lives of the Catholic clergy.

He thanked his priests for their service, calling them 'one of his gifts from the Lord'. 'Not once in my life as a bishop,' he said, 'has a priest refused to undertake a role I offered, no matter how arduous or demanding ... since Vatican II life has become more serious but we have never lost our collective sense of humour and even in the saddest of circumstances, there is still the ability to laugh, the ability to love life, to feel fulfilled, to take a long, loving look at what is, and to say *Deo gratias.*'

Morale-boosting words, but they were not enough to sustain Father Noel Barry through the aftermath of the court case. Some months later he was reported in the *Scottish Catholic Observer* as being 'on indefinite leave', and left to practise his priestly ministry elsewhere.

Nor, away from the atmosphere of mutual appreciation at the City Halls, did the cardinal's words take away the feelings of disappointment which many people – among both clergy and laity – were nursing.

Cardinal Winning has adopted a stoic attitude: priests will have to live with the injustice of being defamed as a consequence of the few who have had a 'bad press' and grow stronger through the pain of it. He believes that any damage which has been done to the priest-people relationship as a result of the 'scandals' will be mended but the clergy, like other professionals, have to be ever-conscious of the boundaries between themselves and others, while still retaining the regard and affection they should have for the people in their charge.

The perception of a priesthood 'in crisis' means that few Catholic parents advocate it as a career choice for their sons nowadays. They know that for every priest who drops out or makes the headlines because of a fall from grace, there are many others who live out their difficult vocations as best they can and do sterling work in the community. But being a priest no longer has the same kudos as it had in Tom Winning's young days more than fifty years ago.

So does this mean that Cardinal Tom Winning is the captain of a sinking ship? He does not think so.

He remembers the days when there were four or five priests in every parish. One or two would always be able to hide behind the rest. Now they are all in the front line, getting responsibility for looking after a community much sooner than before. He remembers calculating the number of 'casualties' who left the priesthood after Vatican II. It struck him that the earlier men were given responsibility, the less likely they were to give up.

It is as if the life of the priest nowadays has become more demanding, more authentic for each one of them. The numbers might be leaner but the work force is keener, as they do not have to wait around for thirty years to step into dead men's shoes, as they did in the past, in order to get a parish.

Those who do become priests nowadays are ordained at a much later age than in the past, giving them an opportunity to experience life and ensure that they have really thought about the nature of their commitment. The cardinal hopes that this will lessen the drop-out rate in the future: fewer priests but better prepared priests to 'man' the parishes.

'Man' seems to be the operative word. John Paul II will not consider women priests. But if the time should come in Scotland when priests will all have to minister to more than one parish, does Tom Winning think that celibacy should be abandoned and priests allowed to marry in order to swell the ranks?

No. He does not believe that the church should give up the tradition of a celibate priesthood, seeing it as a sign, in a sex-obsessed society, that there is more to life than physical gratification, that it is still possible for men to make sacrifices for the sake of the kingdom of God. The influx of married Anglican clergy into the church, as more and more of them convert to Catholicism in England and Wales, is bound to have an effect on the celibate priests, he does admit, but as he has always done throughout his church career, Tom Winning agrees with the Pope. Celibacy should remain and the laity play more of a role in the future as catechists and ministers of the eucharist, just as they do in developing countries, to assist a pared-down clergy.

The paradoxical phrase 'less is more' is often used in the world of fashion. Recently, it has seemed apt to apply it to the Archdiocese of Glasgow. Mass attendance has fallen there as it has everywhere else over the years, yet since 1993, those who have attended the Glasgow churches have helped the cardinal to get out of his financial crisis. A debt of £9.7 million has been completely cleared. £4.8 million has been contributed by parishioners at 'second collections' during Sunday Masses all over the city with the remaining shortfall being made up by sales of church land and general cost-cutting. Another five-year plan has been drawn up to ensure that the archdiocese lives within its means. Its social welfare programme, however, continues to expand.

In 1997, Cardinal Winning told women throughout Britain who might be considering having abortions, to rethink, to choose life and not death for the babies they were expecting and come to the archdiocese for help if they required it. He did not ask anyone for assistance, financial or otherwise. Yet hundreds of thousands of pounds have been contributed to assist the mothers in need.

Having weathered the storms caused by the exposés which beset the church at the end of the nineties, and approaching his seventy-fifth year, maybe Cardinal Winning would decide, at last, to 'keep his head down' and retire from the limelight? He did neither of these things. In his effort, as he saw it, to maintain Christian values in Scotland, Tom Winning developed an even higher public profile instead.

2000 – and the church's calendar was crammed with celebratory events to commemorate the birth of Christ. Cardinal Winning sent a letter to every Catholic household in the Archdiocese of Glasgow encouraging families and individuals to give more effective witness to the Christian faith. 'We need the courage that comes from acting together to make the Word of God a force for change in our communities,' he wrote to them. 'It is our privilege to carry with us, wherever we go, the message that Jesus is alive! It is in our hearts, it is on our lips, it shapes all our behaviour. Living out our baptism means living by this message.'

A new year, a new century, a new millennium. It was not only on the church scene that a feeling of fresh promise had been engendered. There was a new political landscape in Scotland as the country now had its own Parliament in Edinburgh, the first in nearly three hundred years.

Tom Winning had been a guest at the Parliament's official opening by the Queen on 1 July 1999 and was, like his fellow countrymen, full of optimism for its success. The endorsement of devolution by the Scottish people in the referendum two years previously had been decisive. The new Scotland would be a listening Scotland, the nation was told. Legislators would be closer to the people, better able to respond to their concerns. The mood was buoyant.

The Parliament's First Minister, Donald Dewar, carried what Cardinal Winning described as 'a heavy burden for ensuring the future destiny of a country'. A few other MSPs (Members of the Scottish Parliament) were experienced Westminster parliamentarians but the majority were novices in the world of national politics.

Inevitably, there were teething troubles and the Fourth Estate was not slow to criticise when it seemed initially that the main focus of the legislature's attention was the cost of the new Parliament building, holidays, allowances and commemorative medals. The cardinal defended the MSPs publicly, saying that they needed time to establish themselves. Yet the Parliament was not even a year old before Tom Winning was hitting the headlines, declaring it to be 'an utter failure'. 'I am ashamed of our politicians, the way they have behaved and the things they have done over the last year,' he said, in an interview for the *Scottish Catholic Observer* on 2 June, 2000, the day before his seventy-fifth birthday. 'They can talk as much as they like about what they have achieved but in the big issues they have achieved nothing. They have given me the impression that there is a very liberal agenda out there and come hell or high water they are going to see it through.'

The cardinal had been at loggerheads with the new Parliament's Executive, a coalition of the Labour and Liberal Democrat parties, since October, 1999. It was then that the Communities Minister, Wendy Alexander, announced that the legislation which banned the promotion of homosexuality in schools was to be repealed in the Executive's Ethical Standards in Public Life Bill, the following year. The minister described the law as unjust and reactionary and said that it had 'no place in the Scotland of tomorrow'.

The law, Section 2a of the 1986 Local Government Act (commonly known as Section or Clause 28) had been introduced in 1988 because of parental concerns that some local authorities, particularly in London, were spending public money on textbooks designed to promote homosexuality. Clause 28 prohibited local authorities from promoting the teaching, in any maintained school, of the acceptability of homosexuality as a 'pretended family relationship'.

Cardinal Winning had serious concerns about the repeal, which he presented to the First Minister in November, 1999. He told Donald Dewar that if, by the repeal, the Executive wished only to prevent anti-homosexual bullying, then the church would offer its full support. The church condemns homosexual acts as contrary to natural law, but it does not condemn homosexual people. *The Catechism of the Catholic Church* states that they must be accepted with 'respect, compassion and sensitivity' and defended from any form of

discrimination which is unjust. However, the cardinal made it clear
that, in the Catholic Church's teaching, there are areas where it is not
unjust discrimination to take sexual orientation into account: in the
placement of children for adoption or fostering, in the employment
of teachers and in military recruitment.

Cardinal Winning elaborated on his fears concerning a repeal in
an article for the *Scotland on Sunday* newspaper. He was concerned,
he wrote, and, 'if the press reaction is anything to go by', so were
many Scots, 'that any repeal of Clause 28 would open the way to the
teaching of homosexuality, its techniques and its justifications, in our
schools ... any repeal must not leave the way open to a new form of
values-free political correctness which would impose an 'anything
goes' morality on children.'

'I worry that any repeal will be presented by the so-called 'Gay
rights' lobby as a victory in their battle to have the disorder that is
homosexuality placed on the same footing as marriage and family
life,' he continued.

He criticised the Westminster government which, prior to election, had told the country that all legislation would first be given the
'family test' – if a policy did not benefit the family, then it would have
no place on the new government's agenda. But with the lowering of
the homosexual age of consent, the cardinal stated, 'the families of
Britain were left to come to terms with the idea that predatory male
homosexuals would be able to indulge in dangerous, immoral acts
with their sixteen-year-old sons, while our legislators washed their
hands of the whole issue, proclaiming it to be a question of freedom
and equality.' He linked this to the 'current battle' over Clause 28,
stating that if great care was not taken 'we will inadvertently promote
a lifestyle for our children which will reduce their life expectancy,
increase their chances of infection with HIV and expose them to
predatory and abusive relationships.'

'As a church we will make a strong case to the Scottish Executive
for suitable safeguards to be introduced which will protect our children from any attempt at homosexual proselytism,' he concluded. 'I
would caution against any repeal until a set of safeguards have been
put in place.'

In the months which followed, Tom Winning was accused of
many things – but equivocation was not one of them. His views pro-

voked a tremendous reaction and, not surprisingly, a vehement response from homosexual groups. A spokesperson from the Lesbian and Gay Christian Movement described his comments as 'reactionary, unjustifiable, unsubstantiated and anti-Christian'.

But the battle was only just beginning. In January 2000, Mr Brian Souter, a committed Christian and multi-millionaire, offered to finance a campaign by the Scottish School Boards Association to block the Executive's plans to abolish Clause 28. Cardinal Winning publicly supported Souter and the 'Keep the Clause' campaign and called upon the 'silent majority' in the country to 'speak up for their society.' He warned that if there was a repeal, primary and secondary school children faced being exposed to 'explicit and perverted material' which could encourage them to become homosexual.

'It pains me to use the word "perverted" when discussing the homosexual act but that is what it is,' he said. 'Gay rights groups always claim that it is impossible to promote homosexuality. That is rubbish. It is promoted every day by promoting the lifestyles of gay people.'

The Gay Rights activists accused Brian Souter and Cardinal Winning of whipping up intolerance towards gay people and of raising false fears. No one was proposing that children be encouraged to be gay, they said. Their desire was only that schools promote understanding and acceptance to combat bullying of gay and lesbian pupils. Tom Winning was compared to leaders of the Afrikaner Church in South Africa during apartheid. A boycott of Mr Souter's 'Stagecoach' bus company was threatened. Week after week the debate continued in the newspapers – on the front page, in the editorials and in the readers' impassioned letters. Should Clause 28 be repealed or not? As far as the Executive was concerned, it was not a matter for discussion.

The Executive was 'ploughing on', wrote Cardinal Winning in *The Mail on Sunday*, in February, 'in defiance of public opinion. Every neutral test of that opinion shows a huge majority opposed to repealing Section 28. Newspapers have given up running polls on the issue as the results no longer make news.'

The Executive had sent a circular to all Head Teachers in Scotland which indicated that a replacement clause was to be inserted into the Ethical Standards Bill to enshrine family life at the centre of sex education classes. This was to read:

Pupils should be encouraged to appreciate the value of stable family life. At the same time, teachers must respect and avoid causing hurt or offence to those who come from backgrounds that do not reflect this value.

Family values campaigners were not convinced by this proposed 'non-judgemental' clause. Where was the word 'marriage'? Tom Winning described the new proposed replacement for Clause 28 as a 'lowest common denominator fudge': stable family life could, he believed, be interpreted to include homosexual or lesbian domestic arrangements and he feared that the next step would be state recognition of 'so-called' gay marriages.

The cardinal was gloomy. 'Is this what we have come to in the New Scotland, that marriage is so politically incorrect that it cannot be mentioned for fear of offending certain pressure groups?' he said. 'Marriage is not an institution of the church, it comes from natural law. For children, the security and stability of marriage is irreplaceable – yet it is the missing concept from the latest attempt to replace Section 28.'

Scathing in his comments on the Executive, he observed that rather than a people's parliament, the politicians were so out of touch with the genuine concerns of ordinary voters that 'it seemed as if they had been living on a different planet.'

'What are electors supposed to do, what means of expressing their viewpoint remain open to them, when elected representatives stubbornly refuse to listen to their concerns?' Cardinal Winning asked.

Enter Mr Souter again, who decided to finance his own private referendum on whether Clause 28 should be repealed or retained. Enormous posters with the words 'Keep the Clause' appeared on bill boards all over the country. If there were children who had never heard or read about homosexuality before, they were certainly doing so now. Brian Souter was praised and vilified. Some people admired him for his moral crusade, for 'putting his money where his mouth is' and holding a referendum to give the public a chance to express its views. The Scottish Executive described it as a 'flawed opinion poll', pro-repealers said that his referendum was a distortion of democracy, Gay rights campaigners tried to discredit it and encouraged Scots to 'tear up' their voting papers and put them in the bin.

In May, Cardinal Winning offered his public support to Brian Souter again. In a letter to Souter, the cardinal reflected on his hope that the 'new Scotland' 'would have been built on the best of the country's traditions: the family, creativity, humour, openness, hard-work and generosity ... we could never have seen that the marriage-based family would be one of the first casualties.'

Out of 3,970,712 ballot papers posted out to people in Scotland, 1,260,846 valid papers were returned of which 1,094,440 were in favour of keeping Clause 28 and 166,406 in favour of repeal. Both sides of the dispute believed they had been vindicated by the result: the Communities Minister, Wendy Alexander, was quoted as saying that less than one third of Scots backed Souter's position because as time went on, Scots had become increasingly uncomfortable with 'cheque-book democracy'. The 'Keep the Clause' campaigners wondered how, if the government was a listening government, it could fail to ignore the wishes of one million people – a greater number than had put the majority party in Parliament at the election.

Still the Executive was intransigent: the repeal would go ahead. At the end of May, an amendment by Michael McMahon, the Labour MSP for Hamilton North and Bellshill, would have put a clause in the Ethical Standards Bill acknowledging the importance of marriage in raising children while also acknowledging the need to avoid stig-matisation of children from 'alternative family units'. The fears of the 'Keep the Clause' campaigners might well have been alleviated by such a compromise. The amendment was defeated by a Scottish Parliament Committee by seven votes to three.

So the saga continued.

The cardinal received criticism of the stance he had taken from members of his own church, who said he was too abrasive, that he was not showing the love of Christ towards homosexual people, that he did not speak for every Catholic on this matter. His year 2000 message aimed at encouraging people to act together in the church. What encouragement did his words 'disorder' and 'perversion', to de-scribe homosexuality, give to gay and lesbian people to remain in or return to the Christian community?

In response to such criticisms, Cardinal Winning stated that in all his years as both priest and bishop, he had never refused the pastoral resources of the church to any homosexual person who had come to him for advice and support. He knows that a number of Catholics have difficulty in coming to terms with the church's teaching, but does not regret quoting Saint Paul in describing the homosexual act as 'perversion' – an act diverted from its proper purpose. He believes that nowadays too many people cover up harsh realities with euphemisms: 'mercy killing' for euthanasia, 'termination' instead of abortion. The Catholic Church's teaching on homosexual acts is that they are morally wrong and as a cardinal he has no option but to defend that teaching, consistent over the centuries.

The distinction between a person and his actions is fundamental in the Catholic Church and in his archdiocesan newspaper he wrote of its 'abiding care' for homosexual people. However, that compassionate side did not come across during the dispute.

Hundreds of letters were sent to Tom Winning's home and his office, the majority supporting him but, those who did not, disagreeing in the most forceful manner. Parents, particularly mothers, of homosexuals and lesbians, wrote to him telling him how much he had hurt them, feeling that the church was somehow blaming them for their children's homosexuality. He felt nothing but sympathy for these people and understanding of the love they have for their children, but he had not set out to hurt them. He believes they are hurt by their situation, that if their children engage in homosexual acts then that is wrong and no amount of love can make that wrong right. The truth, as Cardinal Winning and the church see it, cannot be suppressed simply because it gives offence.

No matter how firm and unyielding Tom Winning's public persona had been during the eight-month long dispute, he was upset by the comments made about him in the press and did not relish being described as a 'homophobe' and a 'bigot'. Like many others who disagreed with the scrapping of the Clause, he grew to think that those who accused him of being intolerant were themselves more intolerant than anyone else. Was no one entitled to express an opinion which differed from that of the pro-repealers without risking opprobrium?

By mid-June there were signs that the battle was about to end when the Executive at last agreed that any new statutory guidelines would enshrine the special status of parenthood and marriage, and on the 21st of the month the 'Clause' was at last consigned to history.

'An utter failure' had been Tom Winning's summation of the Scottish Parliament's first year and he was immediately taken to task for not differentiating between the Parliament and its Executive. Mr

Alex Salmond, the leader of the Scottish Nationalist Party, was quoted as saying: 'Cardinal Winning has a substantial track record of speaking up for Scotland on poverty, equality and international issues. He should realise that many of us in the Parliament share his views on these issues and want to stand up and be heard.'

The SNP had said that the inclusion of support for the institution of marriage in guidelines to replace Clause 28 was an 'honourable' way out of the deadlock.

Lord James Douglas Hamilton, Conservative MSP, who had shared the cardinal's concerns about the repeal, wrote to him stating that the Executive spoke for itself and not for the Parliament as a whole, while Mr Jim Wallace of the Liberal Democrats said, on the BBC *Question Time* programme, that although he respected the cardinal's right to say what he did, he believed he had got it wrong. Mr Wallace, who was at the time Acting First Minister, thought that the cardinal's view had been very much coloured by the 'Clause' debate and that 'in a quieter moment he would probably be alongside us in trying to end things like rough sleeping and trying to lift children out of poverty.'

But Cardinal Winning had used the word Parliament and not Executive because he did not want to be accused of 'meddling in party politics'. He felt that every single Parliamentarian, not just the Labour and Liberal Democrat MSPs, had a responsibility to meet the aspirations of the people who had put them in Holyrood and, in his opinion, they had singularly failed to do this.

It was not just the repeal of Clause 28; there were other issues concerning him, such as the moves to make divorce easier, legislation dealing with the rights of incapacitated adults which could 'well open the back door to euthanasia'. These, according to Cardinal Winning were part of the politicians' 'liberal agenda' which it was up to society to reject.

* * *

Cardinal Winning has been both admired and reviled for his outspoken style. His own people love him when he speaks up for the underdog and when he comes out fighting against anyone who unfairly criticises the church or tries to erode what he considers to be moral and spiritual values. They are proud of him when he represents them at serious national occasions, like the funeral of Diana, Princess of Wales, and the service held in memory of the people who were killed in the bombing at Omagh, in Northern Ireland.

But they don't like him when he criticises Catholics themselves and makes them feel uncomfortable – as when he told them that theirs was not a 'pick 'n' mix' church in which they could select the parts of it that they liked and ignore the rest. You send your children to a Catholic school – but do you go to Sunday Mass? You say you are a good Catholic, but what do you do for your parish community? He always challenges.

He is a practical man who has led his archdiocese through one of the most turbulent periods in the church's history. He was instrumental in bringing the Pope to Britain, largely through the force of his persuasive personality and, although only time will tell how effective his pastoral plan has been, Tom Winning has succeeded in changing attitudes within his church in ways which no-one would have believed possible a quarter of a century ago.

His main aim has been to stem the 'tide of secularism', as he calls it, and keep God at the heart of people's lives.

The boy from Lanarkshire, who always said he had no ambitions to rise through the ranks in the church, managed to do just that. The chances of his going any further? That question has been debated both long and hard. Has the man himself ever expressed any views on the subject? Would he be ready, willing and able to take on such a job?

Many years ago, as auxiliary bishop, Tom Winning was giving a talk in a parish hall in Glasgow. Suddenly, in the middle of the speech, with a comedian's timing and his customary grin, he whisked off the purple skull-cap he had been wearing on his head and turned it inside out to reveal a pure white lining. People were laughing even before he began to speak. 'In case of quick promotion!' he said.

That's Winning.